UFOs & OUTER SPACE MYSTERIES
a sympathetic skeptic's report

UFOs & OUTER SPACE MYSTERIES
a sympathetic skeptic's report

BY

JAMES E. OBERG

Donning
Norfolk/Va. Beach

Chapter Five originally appeared in *OMNI* magazine, August 1980, and is reprinted with permission; Chapter Six is an updated version of an article which originally appeared in *FATE* magazine, and is reprinted courtesy of the Clark Publishing Company. Chapters One and Two originally appeared in *True UFOs and Outer Space;* Chapters Eight and Nine originally appeared in *SAGA's UFO Report;* Chapter Four appeared in *Search* (Palmer Publications); Chapter Seven appeared in *The Skeptical Enquirer.* The introduction is a speech presented at *OMNI's* "UFO Summit" in 1979; a condensed version won the 1979 Cutty Sark UFO Essay Prize. The Afterword is based on a speech given at the 1980 Smithsonian UFO Colloquium.

Photographs are courtesy of NASA, plus:
p. 165 Colman Von Keviczky
p. 74 Ivan Sanderson estate
p. 109 Center for UFO Studies
p. 94 101 Lunar Photos
p. 177 Jukka Mikkola
Lunar and Planetary Institute

For information, write: The Donning Company/Publishers, 5659 Virginia Beach Boulevard, Norfolk, Virginia 23502.

Library of Congress Cataloging in Publication Data

Oberg, James E., 1944-
UFOs and space phantoms.
Bibliography: p.
  1. Unidentified flying objects. I. Stine, Hank.
II. Title.
TL789.023   001.9'42   81-3193
ISBN 0-89865-102-6 (pbk.)   AACR2

TO EVERYONE WHO HAS EVER LOOKED OUTWARDS AT THE STARS AND WONDERED . . . .

Table of Contents

INTRODUCTION

Suggestions from a Sympathetic Skeptic

Right up front, let me say that I do not believe that thirty years of UFO reports have proven the existence of something "beyond current human understanding." That point of view is bound to be about as welcome as Banquo's ghost at MacBeth's feast, termites at a carpenters' convention, or a mother-in-law on a honeymoon. UFO skeptics are generally regarded as some vague combination of Ebenezer Scrooge, Darth Vader, Grumpy the Dwarf, and the current president of the Flat Earth Society.

I am not a habitual unimaginative skeptic. I look with interest on stories about the Loch Ness monster and about dowsing, and have a weakness for near-death out-of-body reports and reincarnation stories. As a third-generation Swedish-American, I'm a firm believer in the Kensington Rune Stone. I believe in the Warren Commission Report and in the reality of the energy crisis. I'm an enthusiast for outer space expansion, I've written a book on rebuilding and colonizing other planets, and I feel quite convinced that interstellar travel is possible—but don't ask me for details for another century or two.

I admit I have nothing against fictional space aliens such as Superman from the vanished planet Krypton, Mr. Spock from Vulcan, Mork from the planet Ork, or the coneheads. Since the days of Voltaire's *Micromegas*, extraterrestrial visitors have enriched our literature and our philosophy, and have given us new insights into our own foibles as well as a lot of laughs.

1

And yet I don't "believe" in UFOs. UFO skeptics are in bad repute these days. Pontificating PhDs quick to denounce something as 'impossible' have given science a bad name. Mocking friends and neighbors, quick to ridicule someone's amazing story, have often silenced potentially valuable witnesses. Know-it-all government spokesmen, assuring a concerned public that the situation is well in hand, have lost all credibility. UFO enthusiasts have been entirely justified in disputing such ill-informed knee-jerk skepticism.

However, for the new breed of so-called "informed skeptics" —people conversant with UFO literature, familiar with the multi-faceted aspects of UFO experiences, and well versed in research techniques—for these people the UFO movement has reserved a very special circle of Hell, that would have made Dante proud. True, in public, UFO experts call for cooperation from skeptics (as long as the skeptics don't disagree too insistently with them); true, in private, many leading UFO experts carry on friendly and productive relationships with skeptical researchers. But the UFO literature consistently characterizes non-believers as the ignorant, the unimaginative, the intellectually cowardly, or, worse, deliberate or duped agents of deception on the part of the government, the UFO masters, or some other secret group.

Well...yup, that's me. I've seen the evidence for UFOs and I'm not convinced. What it has convinced me of is that there is so much unreliable data being processed that any product it might produce is meaningless; it has so convinced me that the canonized miracles of UFO dogma are riddled with error and fraud; and I've been forced to reluctantly conclude that leaders of the UFO movement are generally unable to grapple with the philosophical bases of their would-be scientific revolution, and are not likely to do so in the foreseeable future.

If I really were a dyed-in-the-wool skeptic, I'd look at the current pitiful state of UFOlogy and I'd be chortling with glee. If I really were part of a hypothetical coverup, I'd rest in smug satisfaction that our secrets were safe—nobody would recognize them if they stumbled across them, and if they did, the data would be trumpeted by spokesmen already so discredited by decades of crying "wolf!" that nobody would pay any attention.

But I'm not gleeful or smug—I'm sadly disappointed. I think UFO reports are well worth studying, at the very least for psychological reasons. I also think that popular attitudes towards UFOs are well worth studying, at this time at the very least for sociological reasons. There may be a chance, however remote, that something worthwhile will be directly or indirectly discovered—and I think that such a possibility both justifies continued interest and demands better standards. So that is where I see the contribution of the sympathetic skeptic to UFOlogy: to proclaim the justification of such continued work, and the need for public cooperation, as well as to enforce higher scientific standards by calling "foul!" when it's required.

It's a thankless task, mainly, but an intellectually stimulating one. There have been too many easy UFO targets for serious skeptics to explain away: too many unchecked facts; too many ignored solutions; too many unsound conclusions; too many illogical assertions. It was, in short, too easy to score points! But I'm glad to say it's getting just a little bit harder. UFOlogy is better for this trend—I'd like to see it continue.

At present, UFO research seems to be at a crossroads. Some UFOlogists have resolutely set off in the direction of scientific standards, while others pay lip service to this ideal but pull back in anguish when they see too many of their favorite UFO stories and theories fall victim to better-equipped researchers. Other UFO theorists are descending into paranoid fantasies in which the whole UFO phenomenon is seen as a deliberate attempt to brainwash the human race. The spaceship enthusiasts (the so-called "nuts-and-bolts" school) have turned from a fascinated flirtation with hypnosis-extracted reports of UFO kidnappings to a now no longer disreputable search for the Holy Grail of UFOdom, the "secret stashed crashed saucer" which, together with the pickled bodies of its dead alien crew, is being sqirreled away somewhere by our government (or the Norwegian government, or the Bolivian government, or by somebody, anybody).

The way in which UFO specialists deal with these diverse trends, and deal with the gadfly pesterings of the skeptics, will demonstrate whether or not UFOs ever become a topic for reputable science, or whether UFOlogy will fade from its present high water mark in popular esteem and subside into the company of crackpot cults such as the hollow earthers, Bermuda tri-angulation, the creationists, the ozone energy buffs, and other groups whose hey-day came and went. To avoid such a fate, UFOlogy must grapple with some essential questions which promise to deliver unpleasant answers.

*****

Where after all should lie the burden of proof of UFOs? This question is central to judging whether or not UFOlogy is a science, a proto-science, an unborn science—or just a hysterical pregnancy.

3

The heart of the scientific method is that extraordinary claims demand extraordinary proofs. Again: *extraordinary claims demand extraordinary proofs.* The accusation (and such it is) that our present understanding of the universe cannot account for certain data must be established without a shadow of a doubt. Those claimants for extraordinary stimuli behind some UFO reports must themselves establish that no conventional explanations are possible. "Science" is represented by a 'defense attorney' who only needs to show reasonable doubt to foil the case of the 'prosecutor' who speaks for UFOlogy.

Yet certain UFO spokesmen have completely reversed this time-tested procedure, attempting to sidestep their responsibilities. UFOlogists have denied that conventional rules should apply to this field, complaining that scientists are prejudiced when they try to apply the same rigorous standards to UFO reports, that they have demanded of their own work over the years.

Here in my view, then, is how scientific methodology has become perverted by UFOlogists posturing as aggrieved victims, parties against whom accusations have been made. They see skeptics as 'prosecutors' who, by being required to *disprove* UFO data, must establish the sufficiency of today's science in the face of UFO reports. Some UFOlogists, on the other hand, try to assume for themselves the role of defense attorneys for these extraordinary claims, which, if not disproved, must be accepted as fact.

And I feel that this subtle switching of roles, this abdication of the responsibility of proof, is a perversion of the scientific method. It is not science, it does not produce real evidence—it is a sterile dead end that will only lead to intellectual disasters and public humiliation for UFOlogy.

Here again, the barren fields of UFOlogical theory are clearly evident. Another key element of a true scientific theory is its ability to be disproved, or its "falsifiability." Most UFOlogists only pay lip service to this essential requirement: that anyone coming up with a new theory has the unavoidable responsibility of preparing experiments by which data can be obtained, which will either fulfill the theory's predictions or will prove it wrong.

Yet this has never happened with UFOlogy. Innumerable anecdotes have been collected and collated with the most modern data processing techniques. Innumerable speculations have been voiced, published, and argued over. None of these speculations have ever deserved the name "theory," since none of them has ever been formulated so as to be disprovable. UFOlogists, when pressed, may sadly admit that even with the often and loudly proclaimed progress and impending breakthroughs in their field, they are today no closer to good theories about the phenomenon than they were thirty years ago, or was Charles Fort fifty years ago. This should be a hint: the very foundation of the field is faulty.

*****

One of the mainstays of UFOlogy's claim to legitimacy is the purported existence of a residue of unsolved and essentially unsolvable UFO reports, whose presence can be explained only by postulating the consequent existence of an extraordinary stimulus (i.e., a phenomenon beyond the understanding of contemporary scientific knowledge). This stimulus might be due to extraterrestrial spacecraft—this is still the most popular suggestion but it is on the wane—or to postulated psychic projections, interdimensional apparitions, time machines, secret human technologies, or "Something Else."

I submit that the attempt to prove a positive based on the possible existence of a negative—the inability to solve every case—is totally illogical, and furthermore that any subject which attempts to base its existence on such justification is founded on fallacy. Yet this claim appears to be the central pillar of the UFOlogical universe.

I call this the "residue fallacy." Its illogic may be made more apparent by rewording it in reverse form. It then reads this way: *If every UFO report were based solely on prosaic, understandable stimuli, then therefore amateur UFO investigators would be able to reliably solve every such UFO report.*

Based on everyday experience with real people and events, that assertion can clearly be seen to be nonsense. Every crime is not solved, every missing person is not found, every air crash is not explained—but we do not feel the need to conjure up alien criminals, alien kidnappers, alien plane killers. Just so with UFOs: there will always be an artificial residue, induced purely by bizarre coincidences, by limitations on human perception and memory, by rare undocumented natural occurrences, or by human activities which are never publicized due to military security, to illegality of the activity, or to plain ignorance over the fuss caused by the activity. That residue will never be solved—and no extraordinary stimuli need be referred to. It is a permanent, unavoidable "background noise." This honestly generated residue, by the way, does not even require the existence of very clever hoaxes, which also plague UFO investigators because their psychological motivations are often extremely obscure. ("Why *should* they lie?" Investigators demand of skeptics, ignoring much of what we know of human behavior.)

Looking at it in another way, consider the tremendous volume of UFO reports, the vast majority of which are acknowledged to be based on honest misperceptions. (The small minority of spectacular hoaxes attracts disproportionate attention.) These we call "identifiable flying objects" or IFOs: the "IFO" category may be 90%, 95%, 98%, or even higher.

Now imagine this thought experiment: let the subset of UFO reports based on truly extraordinary stimuli (if any) be removed from the total class of all reports. For example, suppose for one whole year that there were no real UFO stimuli. Would the UFO reports, which would continue practically unabated based purely on the IFO "background noise," look any different? Would we then be able to solve all of those reports?

I think the answer to both questions is "no." That is, we are unable to distinguish between a situation in which there may be true UFOs and an artificial situation in which there are no true UFOs at all. If these two situations appear the same, I suggest they may really be the same.

So I maintain that the statistical approach to proving the existence of UFOs is bankrupt because of faulty bookkeeping. The much-touted "unsolved cases" fraction by itself proves nothing.

*****

Not let's get into specifics. Avoiding broad generalizations and handwaving, let's see if specific cases can prove the need to admit the existence of extraordinary stimuli for UFO reports.

UFO experts do not appear to like being put on the spot to be specific, to designate actual individual reports as "unsolvable." This viewpoint would give skeptics the opportunity to narrow their fire and concentrate on cases certified by top UFOlogists as unsolvable. As a leading UFO specialist said in 1975: the UFO evidence is most convincing when, like a bundle of sticks, considered *en masse*. Of course, his analogy tacitly implies that individual UFO cases, like individual sticks, can be easy to "break"; and suggests that the evidence for UFOs will stand up only if it is not investigated too closely. While not a very flattering portrait and clearly not what the speaker intended, it may have been right on the money.

What are the "best cases?" There are some classics (and I've treated many of them in my Column in *Omni*), but many of these are now too far in the past to ever be properly investigated. Of contemporary cases, the most famous selection has been made annually by a "Blue-Ribbon-Panel" of UFO experts sponsored by the *National Enquirer*, which awards cash to the "most scientifically valuable" report each year from 1972 to 1980.

The 1972 best case involved a farm family in Delphos, Kansas, who reported a close encounter with a UFO which left a mysterious ring on the ground. Subsequent chemical analysis (unpublished) showed that the circular mark was a fungus fairy ring; the family, meanwhile, later came up with new stories of anniversary UFO return visits, and of a presumably unrelated encounter with a "wolf girl." I think the original story, too, is a tall tale.

The 1973 best case was an encounter between an Army helicopter crew and a nightflying UFO. I wrote this case up in one of my *Omni* columns; it's one of the best ever, despite the record of unreliable testimony from flight crews in general. Unfortunately, their descriptions lead me to believe the case is based on honest misperception of either a fireball meteor or an illegally hotrodding military jet; however, over the years the case has grown in the retelling and the present version is truly miraculous—it has, however, little in common with what was originally reported.

The 1974 best case was a combined radar-visual sighting at the San Antonio airport. Ray Stanford investigated the case and showed it was definitely a hoax by two teenagers who launched a flare balloon (the police recovered the balloon). The UFO media has scrupulously avoided publishing Stanford's conclusions.

The 1975 best case was the reported abduction of Travis Walton of Snowflake, Arizona. Subsequent investigation by Philip J. Klass of *Aviation Week* revealed compelling motivations for fraud, and turned up the fact that although Walton flunked a polygraph test right after his alleged release, that fact was covered up and even denied outright by UFO investigators. I can't help but think the case is a hoax.

The 1976 best case was an encounter between Royal Iranian Air Force jets and several UFOs in the air over Tehran. The case has up to now never really been investigated and was probably picked because it never could be investigated properly, and hence is immune from being solved. There are some facts dealing with Iranian politics that suggest that it was a misperception and coincidence compounded by a coverup by higher ranking officers and officials.

7

The 1977 best case was a triangular UFO in the skies over Memphis. (Like all previous cases, this occurrence was also at night). Responsible UFO groups had barely heard of the story until they read about it in the *National Enquirer*, so reliable research has only just begun. I confess I do not know what it was.

And I'm sure we've all heard that Jimmy Carter has seen a

301-949-1267

NATIONAL INVESTIGATIONS COMMITTEE ON AERIAL PHENOMENA (NICAP)®
3535 University Blvd. West
Kensington, Maryland 20795

REPORT ON UNIDENTIFIED FLYING OBJECT(S)

This form includes questions asked by the United States Air Force and by other Armed Forces' investigating agencies, and additional questions to which answers are needed for full evaluatio by NICAP.

After all the information has been fully studied, the conclusion of our Evaluation Panel will be published by NICAP in its regularly issued magazine or in another publication. Please try to answer as many questions as possible. Should you need additional room, please use another sheet of paper. Please print or typewrite. Your assistance is of great value and is genuinely appreciated. Thank you.

1. Name Jimmy Carter   Place of Employment

   Address State Capitol Atlanta   Occupation Governor
                                         Date of birth
                                         Education Graduate
                                         Special Training Nuclear Physics
                                         Military Service U.S. Navy

   Telephone (404) 656-1776

2. Date of Observation October 1969   Time ___ AM 7:15 PM Time Zone EST

3. Locality of Observation Leary, Georgia

4. How long did you see the object? Hours ___ Minutes 10-12 ___ Seconds ___

5. Please describe weather conditions and the type of sky; i.e., bright daylight, nighttime, dusk, etc. Shortly after dark.

6. Position of the Sun or Moon in relation to the object and to you. Not in sight.

7. If seen at night, twilight, or dawn, were the stars or moon visible? Stars.

8. Were there more than one object? No. If so, please tell how many, and draw a sketch of what you saw, indicating direction of movement, if any.

Jimmy Carter's UFO report was filed in 1973. By that time he had forgotten where and when he'd seen the UFO; other details were probably similarly distorted.
Photograph credit NICAP

8

UFO, too. UFO spokesmen and the UFO media have never tired of repeating this assertion. Yet how many of us are aware of the fact that of all the experts who use this story not one has actually investigated the case to see if it is a "real UFO" or, as is more likely, one of the 90% or more IFOs? More, does anyone suspect as I do that these UFOlogists have deliberately avoided such investigations out of fear that some prosaic solution might actually be found, ruining a useful publicity gimmick?

One man did check the story out, and he revealed gross errors in the published accounts and isn't it funny how errors seem to always occur in the direction of more mystery rather than that of solution? According to skeptical investigator Robert Sheaffer of Santa Cruz, California, even the dates of the event have been distorted, usually by months, sometimes by three or four years. Sheaffer attributes the original sighting to a misperception of Venus, whose unexpected brilliance over the night horizon has fooled pilots, politicians, missionaries, scientists, and even astronauts. While personally I do find his hypothesis compelling, the validity of the hypothesis is not the issue I want to raise. Instead, it is the irresponsibility of those who would exploit the story with no regard for its authenticity that is important, since it casts disrepute on the entire science of UFOlogy.

Next: we are also told that the United Nations has encouraged and endorsed research into UFOs. This is in fact one of the most tawdry and *embarrassing* affairs in recent UFO history, involving political expediency that would have made Machiavelli wince. As described in a column in 1979, the UN UFO *debacle* was fueled solely by the fanaticism of the crackpot president of a small Caribbean island (who was subsequently overthrown in a Coup D'etat and is now missing) and by *the ambitions* of UFO experts who sought to cloak themselves in the respectability of the world organization.

The only reason that UFOs ever came before the UN is that Eric Gairy, late of the small island nation of Grenada, used his diplomatic privileges to foist an unwelcome subject upon an unwilling host. Early in 1978 he *demanded* (as was his right as a head of state) an *audience* with UN *Secretary-General* Kurt Waldheim, and then brought in tow a passle of hand-picked UFO experts as part of *his* own entourage. Subsequently, participants at this brief courtesy call have made glowing references to this "top UN UFO meeting", this "closed UN conference", this "breakthrough in international recognition of the seriousness of the worldwide UFO problem", and similar nonsense—completely and deliberately misrepresenting the nature of the trivial event.

The great un-UFO debacle of 1978-1979 was based on the attempted mutual exploitation by madcap dictator Gairy and an assortment of American UFO experts who privately despised him but publicly embraced him to gain a prestigious forum. Photograph and postage stamp courtesy of MUFON

Along the way, they also embraced Gairy as a courageous diplomat, while mocking him in private.

Then in November, again at Gairy's insistence, (as was his perogative as a head of state) a UFO discussion was added to the agenda of the Special Political Committee. The committee heard from Gairy's delegation (which consisted of numerous well-known UFO figures) and politely passed the buck. But when Gairy was suddenly sacked, the topic was quickly dropped in

UFO proponents have frequently touted this photo as portraying a "closed UN Conference on UFOs." Actually, UFO crackpot Sir Eric Gairy of Grenada insisted on his right to a courtesy call on Kurt Waldheim, and brought along a group of UFO experts as part of his private entourage. Waldheim never invited them back. (July 14, 1978). Photograph courtesy of the United Nation and taken by Sam Lwin

its entirety.

The UFO movement was left with some nice headlines, some phony character references, and some private embarrassments— but don't expect to see this version of the UN affair in the UFO press.

Few books, 'documentaries,' or lectures on UFOs go by without at least passing references to the claim that "Astronauts have seen UFOs too." Together with standard claims of government coverup, these stories can be assembled to spell out details of more than forty incidents in which space pilots have allegedly seen and photographed unidentified flying objects in space (including ten on Apollo-11 alone!).

In fact all the reported "astronaut UFO" incidents, upon careful investigation, fall into one of several categories. First and most numerous are the hoaxes (not by astronauts themselves), where unscrupulous sensationalists, counting on the gullibility of UFO enthusiasts, misword voice transcripts (or make them up entirely) and mislabel prosaic photographs (or forge them by retouching). And by the way, there are virtually no risks to these deceptions, since before I personally checked these stories nobody else had—or at least had not published negative results. Even when caught, the hoaxers have done nothing illegal. They've now gotten rich or famous and besides, the public either won't be told about the exposure or they won't believe it anyway!

Second, most numerous are the ordinary space events misunderstood by outsiders and subsequently dramatized incorrectly to make "good UFO stories." These are often based on sightings and photographs of ice flakes off the spaceship's fuel tanks, sightings of cast-off boosters and similar spent hardware, or photographs which show anomalous lighting effects due to dirty windows, lens flares, or similar all too common amateur photographic problems.

Lastly are the handful of reports of genuine interest, which, even when solved, can still be remarkably eerie. On Apollo 12, for example, the astronauts were baffled by a diffuse bright light which appeared to be hanging between them and the earth. (It turned out to be the moon's reflection off the nighttime Indian Ocean forty thousand miles below.) On Gemini 4, there is Jim McDivitt's brief glimpse of a 'beercan shaped' object which he thinks was another satellite but still insists should be called a "UFO" (I checked into the case and suspect it was a glimpse of his own castoff booster rocket, which is known to have been nearby and was shaped like a beer can). On Gemini 11 there was a sighting and photographs of a passing satellite that NORAD radar control says was the Russian Proton 3 — but which subsequent orbital analysis has shown could not have been. (I think it was some other man-made satellite, but there are too many to check).

These encounters, while not providing any useful information about UFOs, allow UFO enthusiasts to continue to boast that "astronauts have seen UFOs too." *This is False.* Nothing seen or photographed by astronauts has turned out to have any value for UFOlogical science, except in studying how gross hoaxes and errors can spread unchecked for year after year, but they sure provide good publicity gimmicks, which, as far as this type of story is concerned, is all that UFO buffs appear to have ever been interested in.

*****

Based on the authenticity of this kind of data, why are UFOs so popular? For the media, of course, UFO stories are good business. They combine human interest, comic relief, and occasional scary stories, with popular swipes at "smart-ass college scientists" and "government coverups." It has been well established that public attitudes about UFOs have been shaped by irresponsible (and profitable) journalism in the weekly tabloids, in the UFO and occult pulp magazines, in books, in TV dramatic series, and in the broadcast media in general—all using such popular techniques as repeating and embellishing unchecked rumors, withholding explanatory facts and subsequent solutions ("it's not news anymore"), interviewing the wildest-sounding spokesmen, and so forth.

This is not a judgment on the validity of what is called "the real UFO phenomenon," only on what the public knows about UFOs, or thinks it knows about UFOs. So to say that the majority of Americans now think that "UFOs are real" is to testify not to the strength of the UFO evidence but only to the effectiveness of the media mythmakers.

Prominent UFOlogists will privately admit this and decry the sensationalism and exploitation of the news media. Yet in public they boast of the fact that most Americans now "believe" in UFOs. In a Biblical metaphor, they savor the fruit while cursing the tree.

The motivation of UFO enthusiasts is also a subject worthy of close study. Many are driven by a commendable scientific curiosity and an honest conviction that UFO research may contribute significantly to human knowledge and/or wisdom. I personally wish them well. UFO study is also one of the few fields of scientific inquiry still open to amateurs.

However, for many other UFO buffs, their interests are, in my opinion, fuelled by less noble motives. Some seem to be on ego trips, exulting in a world of fantasy where they form an elite knowledgeable vanguard of free-thinkers, superior to cocky scientists, mocking neighbors and relatives, and unsympathetic teachers. For others, their very rejection is sensed by them as proof of their virtue and rectitude. That they are persecuted, or what they think is persecution, places them in the company of great scientists and thinkers of the past who had to overcome ancient dogmas to establish new truths. I call this latter the "Galileo Complex."

It is, of course, a total fallacy—although nearly every UFO book, magazine, speech and interview makes reverent reference to it. Being laughed at (or even being jailed, as in the past) does not make you right. The vast majority of "scientific revolutionaries" who claimed to be the prophets of new sciences turned out to be the crackpots they appeared to be; the upwards trail of science is littered with the wreckage of crackpot theories which utterly deserved the scorn and hostility they received. The success rate of scientific revolutions is depressingly low, although our history books generally list only the successes, giving the thoroughly false impression that the outsiders were usually right and stodgy establishment dinosaurs were usually wrong. This impression fuels the 'Galileo Complex,' but it is counterfeit.

There's also a pseudo-religious aspect to UFO enthusiasts, as well—the notion of benevolent saviors from the sky is too obvious an image to require any comment. I do not want to dwell on the regrettable fact that the UFO field has attracted more than its fair share of cranks and cultists, since this should not be a criterion for judging the authenticity of UFOlogy itself. Other fields—medicine, politics, economics, religion, education— attract cranks and cultists too, but I must say that most of them seem to police themselves somewhat more efficiently.

*****

A fair question to demand of skeptics is to describe what kind of evidence would be required to convince them that "UFOs are real" (even though, when tables are turned, UFO believers will not describe corresponding criteria for "disproof"). I think that many so-called proofs already on the record books would have been convincing if they had turned out in reality to be nearly as impressive as they were in print. Physical proof could include materials beyond the manufacturing capability of modern indus- try, or biological specimens exhibiting an unearthly biochemis- try. Informational proof could be in the form of astronomical or other knowledge unknown to contemporary science, but subse- quently confirmed (and there have been some teasers here). Instrumental proof would include separate photographers, coor- dinated and reliable multi-instrumental readings, or similar untouched-by-human-hands recordings. And surely this is not too much to expect—yet neither the *National Enquirer* prize, a 1979 one million pound sterling prize from Cutty Sark Ltd. in London, or NASA's offer of the use of its laboratories has so far brought such evidence to the surface.

And what of the future? Where is UFOlogy likely to be ten, twenty, or thirty years from now? In my heart, I think I'm still rooting for the success of these scientific revolutionaries, and I'm sure *I'd be delighted* to see breakthroughs in physics, physiology, biology—or the legendary "first contact" with extraterrestrials. Indeed, insofar as my criticisms can tighten up the standards of UFOlogy, I will lay claim to (but doubtlessly will be denied) a share of the credit for whatever such invigorated studies produce.

14

This is my personal desire.

But in more realistic (and cynical) moments I rate such feelings the same way Samuel Johnson reportedly (according to his biographer Boswell) rated the news of a friend's second marriage, "Ahh," he is quoted as say, *the triumph of hope over experience.*"

Whatever the outcome of such investigations, UFO stories will always hold a fascination for imaginative, space-minded people.

In recent years I hope that I have helped contribute a new dimension to that fascination by providing intriguing narratives of "detective stories" in which careful investigation has revealed the actual facts behind many famous UFO incidents. And even when the UFO itself may be shown to be bogus, the fascination remains—because the spread and growth of each "Legend of Space" is a worthy study by itself, regardless of the actual origins of the legends.

So now we will track down many of the best-known UFO space encounters: The astronaut sightings, the mysterious activity on the moon; The Betty and Barney Hill story; and other examples from UFO literature and from intellectually allied space-related fields—such as primitive tribes with apparently modern astronomical knowledge, and the Soviet Spaceflight frauds and coverups. In each case we will dig deeply and unrelentingly in pursuit of the thread of truth, all the way to the roots. This will always be informative and eye-opening. So bring on the mysteries of the Space Age!

PART ONE
UFOs

Chapter One
UFOs and the Age of Space

The modern age of flying saucers was only a decade old when the space age began. The first UFOs were widely reported in 1947, and the first sputniks went up in 1957. But the world of UFOs and the world of outer space have been closely associated ever since.

According to the dominent "spaceship hypothesis," the UFOs are alien visitors from other worlds. It is therefore reasonable to suspect that they would be very interested in our fledgling space programs, and that our space probes would find traces of the aliens far from earth. Both such expectations have been born out by published reports over the past few years.

Here are some examples of the stories which have connected outer space with UFOs. They form part of a growing body of folklore which is circulated, embellished, and reprinted in the UFO media, among UFO researchers, and on broadcast interviews and other programs. (Although I don't mean to imply that *these* stories have been generally endorsed in the UFO movement. They are merely some of the better known.)

UFOs and the NASA cesium clocks: Late in the 1960s a strange incident was reported from the Kennedy Space Center at Cape Kennedy (now once again Cape Canaveral). Three high-precision cesium clocks, which measure time to the millionth of a second based on the radioactive decay of radio-isotopes, were undergoing testing in preparation for placing one of them in a space probe. One morning a technician was astonished to notice that one of the clocks was deviating from the others by more than two whole seconds!

No known force on earth can alter the rate of radioactive decay, so the researchers reviewed the histories of all three clocks to see if some other factor could have been responsible. On checking the log books, it was discovered that the 'bad' clock had been taken to another facility a mile away for special maintenance during the previous week. This seemed to be a clue, until another technician made some further tests which showed that it was the 'good' pair of cesium clocks which were in error! The 'bad' clock which had been removed for a few days was *correct*. Some accident had distorted *both* other clocks by precisely the same amount! The whole incident was baffling.

Faced with the mystery, one of the technicians admitted that while he was coming to work one night (there were 24-hour shifts in the space program in those days) he had seen a strange glowing object hovering over the building where the cesium clocks were stored. He had not believed his eyes and had refrained from reporting it because he would never be believed and might loose his security clearance. A further check of the records demonstrated that on the night of the UFO sighting the third clock had indeed been in the *other* building and had presumably not been affected by whatever force—deliberate or by-product—was in action connected with the UFO.

UFOs and missing rockets: A routine training launch of an Air Force intercontinental ballistic missile (ICBM) in 1972 suddenly became completely abnormal when the missile disappeared from the tracking equipment after about forty seconds of flight. At first Air Force officials at the California space center thought there might have been a tracking system breakdown, but the equipment proved out to be in perfect working order. The missile had apparently disintegrated completely in mid-air.

A new launch was scheduled the following day, and as the countdown neared zero and the tracking equipment scanned the soon to be filled skies, the Air Force technicians were stupified by an absolutely impossible sight. The "missing missile" had returned to the skies, roaring upwards from the very point at which it had vanished twenty hours before! The new launch was immediately scrubbed and many of the officers ran outside of the blockhouse where they watched the phantom rocket through binoculars. It flew a perfect course and was tracked on islands far out in the Pacific.

Somebody had been 'borrowing' the missile for a whole day.

What could they have wanted with it? And why should they bother to return it in perfect condition when its simple disappearance was becoming accepted. Its reappearance, which was immediately classified Top Secret, might have been some sort of cosmic joke. Who out there is laughing?

UFOs and the Apollo moon shots: One of the strongest facets of UFO lore is the widely accepted fact that all our manned space shots were shadowed by UFOs, and that astronauts brought back dozens of high-quality photographs of alien space vehicles. The most famous UFO incident on a moon shot was during the Apollo-12 voyage in November 1969.

One day out on the three-day earth-moon leg, the astronauts suddenly radioed to Mission Control that two flashing lights had appeared off the bow of their spaceship. While the remarkable aliens beamed some sort of light message at the Apollo, the ground officials tried to figure out what could be causing the sighting.

After rejecting the possibility that the objects could be spinning pieces of the Apollo's booster rocket, the astronaut on earth who acts as radio link (the "capcom") suggested that they could be jettisoned protective panels just lazily tumbling through space. "Gee that could be," replied the astronauts in space, "but one of these lights just shot out here at a tremendous speed." All listeners to the conversation realized that such behavior was impossible for simple space fragments—it had to be an intelligently guided space vehicle of some sort, and it was not from earth.

The Great Galactic Ghoul: Scientists at the NASA Jet Propulsion Laboratory in Pasadena coined this code name for some strange effect which was "gobbling up" Marsbound spacecraft. In the 1960s, a whole series of Soviet and American unmanned space probes were destroyed or badly damaged in a strange zone of space between the earth and Mars.

Oddly enough, there were no hints from on-board instruments that anything around the spacecraft was particularly dangerous. Later probes which successfully negotiated the zone found nothing to account for the events. Yet several hundred million dollars of sophisticated space probes had been 'neutralized' in this zone. Are they in somebody's interstellar museum, or is there a Bermuda Triangle of space?

The tinkered ALSEPS: When Apollo astronauts visited the moon, they sat up atomic powered science stations designed to relay data back to earth from the surface long after the men had returned to earth. These stations were designed for a lifetime of one year, but they have lasted for many years and their nuclear power plants continued to provide electricity far in excess of what was expected.

Early in 1976 one of the ALSEP packages stopped sending radio signals. Its radio receiver had failed the year before but it had continued to transmit local science data without commands from earth. When the radio set finally failed the ground specialists in Houston concluded that the rest of the radio control system had also failed.

A month later, the signals began again! But now the inoperative radio receiver was also working. One puzzled scientist reported, "It was as if someone had just turned the switch back on!" Did someone examine the space hardware, repair it, and do exactly that: turn it back on? If so, they certainly were not from this planet.

The lunar artifacts: Beginning in 1966, space photos from American rockets began showing strange objects on the lunar surface. These included what looked like towers, tracked vehicles, bridges, and other obviously artificial features. Yet despite the thousands of pages of astronaut reports and hundreds of exposed camera film magazines, no hard evidence was ever released. Most observers concluded that the reports were based on misinterpretations and bad guesses.

But in 1975 a retired government worker dropped a UFO bombshell with his publication of thirty five secret NASA photos which show these artificial moon structures. George Leonard has studied the problem for several years and has concluded that, as his book title indicates, *somebody else is on the moon.* The moon is probably the operations base for UFOs seen on earth.

Apollo expeditions were probably secretly motivated, claims such space specialists as Leonard, Don Wilson, and Michael Cohen, to scout out the aliens. The 'scientific' explanations would never have gotten the program out of a congressional committee.

The kidnapped cosmonauts: One of the most tragic chapters in the story of UFOs and the space program is only now coming out. According to amateur space trackers in Europe, they picked up signals from a manned Soviet spaceship way back in 1961. The Vostok ship carried two cosmonauts (a man and a woman) and was not to be announced until after it had broken all previous space records.

But something on the flight went wrong after a week in orbit. Tape recorded messages overheard in Italy and Germany reveal the strange story: an alien space vehicle had closed in with the Vostok spaceship while the astonished and worried space pilots relayed a description to earth. As the UFO came closer, the crew grew frightened. Then, only the static hiss of background radio noise could be heard. The spaceship had vanished, never to be seen again. Moscow, quite understandably, never announced the flight at all.

Reincarnated satellites: Many satellites put into orbit around the earth have functioned for their planned durations and then broken down, only to turn themselves back on a few months or years later. Is there some feature in space which can repair these circuits just as the powers of Uri Geller repair broken watches? Or is some alien intelligence examining the instruments and repairing them for some unknown experiment?

One of the most baffling incidents is connected with a weather satellite which regularly goes dead over the Bermuda Triangle but which then comes back to life once it flies beyond the range of whatever force emanates from that mysterious region of the North Atlantic. The story was not disclosed by NASA but by a professor of engineering at a small Virginia college which had a private satellite tracking station. Other radio amateurs subsequently confirmed the bizarre behavior of the satellite.

What is happening in outer space? What do UFOs have to do with these strange occurrences? What secrets are being withheld by government agencies? And what will a careful examination of these stories tell?

What is the connection between UFOs and outer space?

Many people may think that the space probes to Mars have established the 'fact' that intelligent life could not exist on that planet. I submit that this is not the correct point of view.

What we should be asking ourselves is this: IF there were intelligent life on Mars, life which is the source of the UFO sightings on the earth and the moon, how could *it* make us *think* that Mars was barren, lifeless, and uninteresting? Could we be the victims of a Martian coverup?

After all, dozens of reputable scientists on earth saw and mapped the famous canals on Mars, canals which obviously were irrigation channels designed to support life on a desert world. After all, Soviet scientists have established that the moons of Mars cannot be natural formations, and might just possibly have been constructed by Martians for unknown purposes. After all, just what do space probes tell us about Mars?

Remember that the first American and Russian probes fell victim to the Great Galactic Ghoul and never reached the planet. When American probes did fly past Mars, they passed over some "moon-like" and uninteresting regions, which scientists later discovered were atypical of the planet.

But when the first scout ships arrived to orbit Mars in 1971, what happened? A planet wide dust storm was in progress which completely obscured the view of the surface! Perhaps the Martians were preparing some fake scenery to fascinate earthmen with. When two Soviet space probes entered the Martian atmosphere they mysteriously went dead. They behaved exactly as if they had been shot down by interceptor missiles.

How do we know that the radio data from Mars probes is authentic? It only comes in as pure radio energy. It would not be difficult for an alien civilization to *simulate* the radio signals once they had studied the instruments sufficiently. Is that what was happening during the "dust storm" which blocked our view of Mars in 1971? Because a few months later the storm did appear to clear, showing a barren, lifeless Mars.

Once the Viking probes arrived in 1976, the Mars civilization (I am still only hypothesizing, don't forget) would have time to prepare suitable stage furniture in reserved regions of the planet. Now does it make sense why the television pictures from space prompted scientists to revise their landing points for both probes? The falsified data was leading the Vikings to precisely the points which had been prepared for them. Of course the probes would find nothing of interest!

This is only a hypothesis. It's only one possible explanation. But does it explain all the reported facts as well or better than the 'official' news releases?

Now that the readers have been 'hooked' into wondering if it might be so, I must confess that I do not believe it at all. As a theory, it is fascinating but unsupported by many more facts than can be fitted into a short magazine article.

There are no canals on Mars and there never were any except in the imaginations of astronomers. The moons of Mars are natural objects—they are not hollow space vehicles built by alien civilizations, and the evidence which led Soviet scientists to suggest that theory is faulty. Mars, as seen from earth and from space and from Mars itself, is a very interesting planet, but it is not the home of life forms.

Let us examine each of the "UFOs and Outer Space" stories which I have presented to you and see if there are any more facts which might account for them. We are now going to go further than typical UFO books on the market, because we are convinced that our readers want more than anything the truth. If they wanted fairy tales they could go to the Brothers Grimm or to some other UFO magazine. They want to be treated as adults and not have their intelligence abused.

Somebody told me the story of the cesium clocks at a UFO convention. He had heard it from somebody else. I have no idea where it came from or if it is really true or not. Based on that, I do not believe it and will not believe it until there is more corroborating evidence. But it sure is a good story, and you can see why writers enjoy passing it around. I think it is just that: "a good story".

The same is true for the "missing rocket" story. I was asked about it during a radio talk show, by a very intense young man who seemed to enjoy the stories more than the authentic mysteries. I told him to stick to science fiction if that was what he wanted, but not to pass gossip off as fact. I do not believe the story at all, but it sure is a "good story".

The Apollo moon shot stories are much more interesting. They have appeared in dozens of UFO books, magazines, and on radio and TV shows and in the movies. Space does not permit me to discuss them all but the conclusions are the same: in every case which I have personally investigated, the "UFO sighting" turns out to have been a media exaggeration, misunderstanding, distortion, or outright fabrication. The "transcripts" which allege to portray astronauts describing UFOs are forged. The photos either do not exist, or show something else, or are also forgeries. Many UFO writers seem to have the grossest contempt for the intelligence and trust of their readers to treat them this way.

Take the Apollo 12 case. In this famous incident the initial reports are indeed true, as the astronauts jokingly asked earth about some flashing lights. When told that they were probably tumbling pieces of space debris (which do in fact accompany the Apollo in the vacuum of space on the way to the moon), the crew accepted this and began discussing how far away they would be. When asked how fast the pieces had broken off the rocket the previous day, the astronauts replied that when they had turned their Apollo around some pieces were flying off at a very fast velocity. That had been the day before! The flashing lights visible out the window didn't go anywhere but gradually faded out as the days went by.

What had happened was that UFO researchers (I use the term loosely) had simply misunderstood the space jargon and had completely missed the gist of the conversation from the Apollo, and had then (probably quite honestly, with good intentions and closed minds) reworded the phrases to make them "clearer" to the general public. In fact they had thoroughly altered the meaning, as we shall see later.

The Great Galactic Ghoul was originally an engineer's joke. In fact there is no unique region where the failures occurred. The only thing in common was that they were on very long missions when breakdowns could have been expected—this was in the early days of space flight. The failures occurred at random and were frustrating but hardly mysterious in those days.

The same thing holds for the tinkered ALSEPS. The moon is a very harsh environment with its daytime temperatures and bitter cold nights. As the wires expanded and contracted, they eventually will break, but only intermittently. As they expand again they will make contact again, which is exactly what happened to the ALSEP. Every "lunar afternoon" with temperatures at their highest, the radio came back on. After sunset the signals would stop. After a few months of this the radio wires snapped completely and the station went dead completely.

The lunar artifacts were about as real as the Martian canals. In the shadows and angles of the small, grainy moon photos, some people claimed that they could see squares, crosses, towers, and other features. But as higher quality films came back, the 'features' resolved themselves into natural piles of dirt, rock, and debris.

The most famous artifact probably was the "tower" seen in 1966. In fact, as later analysis showed, it was only a large rock casting a very long shadow soon after dawn. The shadow looked extremely long because it was being cast downhill into a shallow crater, which led to the initial overestimates of the rock's height.

Unfortunately, there is nobody else on the moon. All the photos which Leonard uses to prove otherwise actually show absolutely nothing but the limitless power of the human imagination. Any doubter can buy copies of the films for themselves: NASA, contrary to the UFO claims, has never withheld any space photos from anyone. NASA has even set up a special laboratory called the Lunar & Planetary Science Institute to facilitate the distribution of moon information. Leonard, in researching and writing his book, never visited this center. He did not even know it existed, which shows the depth of his familiarity with lunar research. I will cover this more extensively in chapter four.

The *kidnapped cosmonauts* were born in the publicity-seeking minds of two Italian radio amateurs. Their account is so full of internal contradictions and outright scientific errors that nobody except the late radio-journalist (radio story teller would be a better description) Frank Edwards believed them. But that was enough. Once Edwards had improved on the story and had included it in one of his UFO books, it became firmly entrenched as "fact" rather than "fiction." But fiction it was, a modern space age fable about an event which never really happened.

There is no mystery about 'reincarnated satellites.' Just as on the moon, the alternating hot and cold periods in earth orbits cause circuits to fail in unexpected ways, sometimes causing the snapped wires to fall together again at unpredictable intervals. Many such failures occurred which did *not* entirely cripple the spacecraft, so ground controllers were able to diagnose what was happening. With improved designs of electronics, this has not been a recent problem except in the extreme conditions of the moon.

There remain many mysteries in outer space, and many phenomena which scientists did not expect and which they cannot explain. If it were not so, there would be no point in exploring outer space.

But with more and better data, and with analysis, guesses, and imagination, space scientists are trying to figure what makes the solar system and the whole universe work. It is a fascinating puzzle and the solution will never be complete, as our probes reach new regions of space and send back new unexpected data.

The mysteries of outer space are real, but they have nothing to do with UFOs. If anything, the real space enigmas are far more fascinating and satisfying than any science fiction fables of the 1970s.

Why does Venus rotate backwards, and why is it somehow 'locked' into the earth's position? Why does Uranus rotate on its *side*?

Really, where *did* the moon come from, and what connection does the moon's gravity have with the earth's magnetic field, the earth's continental drift, and the formation of life on earth at all?

What are the strange but apparently natural lights and shadows which do actually occur on the moon's surface? Are they fluorescing gas, electrostaticly levitated dust, or some other diffuse but observable phenomena?

What are the conditions on the outer planetary satellites such as Titan, the new target for the search for extraterrestrial life? Why is satellite Iapatus six times as bright on one side as on the other?

Why? What? How? When? These are the most exciting of days in the exploration of the solar system. A century age we could not hope to find the answers. A century from now we will already have all the answers. This generation alone is blessed with the chance to actually see the answers come in.

There is no need for phony mysteries. Real ones are better.

Chapter Two
Close Encounters—Fact or Fiction?

For years, the claim that some people have met and talked with pilots of flying saucers was greeted with derision and scorn. But the stories kept coming in, so UFO researchers gradually and grudgingly began to examine the claims. They even invented a high-sounding term for such events.

Close Encounters of the Third Kind. The first kind, of course, if you have seen movie ads at all, is a 'UFO sighting.' The second kind involves some sort of physical trace. The third kind is "contact."

These stories continue. They still encounter outright hostility and ridicule and are still met with varying, often contradictory theories and explanations:

Nuts and Bolts: This theory, popular in the 1950s but now fading, claims that the UFOs are spaceships from other worlds, visiting the earth....

Psychic Projections: This theory, gaining ground with the backing of top UFO expert Jaques Vallee, claims that UFOs and encounter stories are images projected into the minds of witnesses by unknown forces....

Delusions and Hoaxes: This classical skeptic's reply, in retreat under the deluge of high-quality contact stories of the 1960s and early 1970s, is on the rise again, spearheaded by the impressive 'debunking' work of arch-UFO-skeptic Philip J. Klass.

Humans and aliens *will* meet someday, out in deep space, or when the alien ambassadors hand over (tentacle over?) their credentials at the White House. But human/alien contact may have already occurred, in the deep and distant past, or in the confused and stormy present. What kinds of "close encounters of the third kind" have been reported?

In 1964, New Mexico policeman Lonnie Zamora saw a UFO land near the highway south of Socorro, New Mexico. According to his story, when he approached, he thought he saw two white-clad figures next to it. The pilots jumped back into the ship, which took off in a blast of flame.

A few years earlier, Betty and Barney Hill were stopped one lonely night on a deserted road in New Hampshire. As revealed under hypnosis later, they were taken on board a UFO and examined. They were shown the UFO's navigation charts, which were later deciphered by astronomers to reveal the alien home base: Zeta Reticuli star system.

In 1973, two fishermen in Pascagoula, Mississippi, were 'levitated' into a UFO by bizarre humanoid creatures. Their story, according to reports, stood up under lie detector tests.

In 1975, a wood cutting party in Arizona was attacked by a UFO which 'zapped' one of the young men and carried him off. He returned, dazed and incoherent but otherwise unharmed, several days later. His story of the UFO base and of his attempted escape is believed to have stood all tests of truthfulness by UFO buffs.

Question: Just *how* can an even-minded investigator determine truth or falsehood in these exceptional and extraordinary stories? The witnesses seem to be sincere and deeply moved by their accounts, yet time and again psychologists have pointed out that such behavior is entirely consistent—indeed, is often a characteristic—with fantasy and "tall-tale-telling."

How about truth tests? We have drugs (thanks to the CIA's illicit experiments), polygraphs (misnamed 'lie detectors'), the new "voice stress analyzer," and hypnotic regression. These techniques may help establish the truth behind these stories.

That is the *fundamental* problem: these are *all* only stories. Corroborative evidence is extremely flimsy. No artifacts have been stolen by the witnesses, even when they have had time to wander through the UFOs, according to their stories. Physical effects on the witnesses are not indicative of any extraordinary experience. Information given to the witnesses by the UFO people, as reported by the witnesses, is usually so nonsensical and valueless that many serious pro-UFO researchers have begun to suspect that the UFOnauts are conducting a deliberate program of misinformation and deception.

And 'second thoughts' among UFO investigators, which might tend to throw doubt on the published UFO close encounter stories, often must be withheld from print since it deals with the characters of the witnesses, often with private matters and neighborhood gossip. Such a problem taints the famous Socorro case, since suspicions of fraud dealing with the financial gain of the owner of the property (who was also the only witness's boss), and other allegations of possible motivations, can be whispered between UFO researchers but cannot be put into print for fear of libel and defamation suits.

A good case in point is the famous ("infamous," perhaps) "Pascagoula kidnapping." The primary witness, Charles Hickson, was reportedly in a very suspicious situation: he had just been fired from his job for extorting loans from subordinates, and had just filed for bankruptcy. Following his UFO story, he hired a press agent who arranged what has been revealed to have been a patently phony 'polygraph test.' Two years later he suddenly backed out of a second, controlled polygraph test.

Hickson reportedly is furious about other people making money off of his sighting, while he has been unable to cash in on a book and movie offer. He's clearly disappointed at the way things turned out.

Late in 1976, an investigator who was upset about Hickson's about face on the controlled polygraph exam attempted to use the new 'voice stress analyzer' system to determine truth or falsehood. The system analyzes harmonics in the voices of witnesses, seeking to detect stress on the vocal cords, stress which is usually associated with intentional lying. The researcher tested a tape of an interview Hickson had made in 1976, three years after the incident, and found no stress. But critics lambasted the results because Hickson had had three years to practice his story again and again: why, the critics asked, hadn't the investigator used tapes made only a few *weeks* after the alleged incident? So the controversy continues.

There is a philosophical issue as well. UFO scientists claim that these "close encounter" stories must be believed until the witnesses can be shown to be liars or hallucinators. Skeptics attempt to reverse the responsibility: they insist that the pro-UFO people must *prove* that the witnesses were *not* liars or hallucinators. Since so much is dependent on the characters of the witnesses, both sides delve deeply into their private lives and reputations. When the skeptics dig up embarrassing information which tends to cast doubt on the total reliability of the witnesses, the pro-UFO people react angrily with charges that the anti-UFO people are trying to "smear" the witnesses with "vicious *ad hominem* arguments" and irrelevent gossip. But that kind of information is at the heart of the credibility of the stories, unfortunately. Such severe publicity probably discourages many witnesses from ever reporting their experiences.

A classic UFO story is the 'New Hampshire abduction' reported by Betty and Barney Hill. Although the event is supposed to have happened in 1961, it did not attain national prominence until the mid-60s when it became the subject of two sales record busting issues of 'Look' magazine, and of a popular book *(Interrupted Journey*, by John Fuller).

In many ways the case set the pattern for innumerable later tales. Basically, a couple on a dark lonely road is frightened by a UFO in the distance, but return home unharmed. It is hours later than it seemed, so they must have lost track of time. Persistent nightmares prompt the husband and wife to seek psychiatric help, and under hypnosis a doctor elicits a startling tale of abduction and examination, a story identical in details in independent testimony by both parties. One of the recalled items of information was the detail of a stellar navigation chart which years later was decoded to point to the star system Zeta Reticuli as the home base of the UFO.

Such a fascinating story could make an impressive and convincing tale—and a dramatic science fiction theme for a movie. In 1975 this is exactly what happened, as NBC-TV produced a made-for-TV movie called 'The UFO Incident'. While fictionalized, it was billed as 'based on facts.'

Two things seemed to happen very quickly after the movie was first shown late that year. First, a skeptical UFO investigator was prompted to dig into the 'Hill case' more deeply— and he soon came up with surprising information which UFO believers would have preferred stayed undiscovered. (Indeed, it later turned out that other pro-UFO investigators had discovered the same information but had stamped their report 'SECRET' and had withheld the information from the public.) Secondly, the TV dramatization of the Hills' story may have planted the seeds of an idea in the mind of a nearly bankrupt Arizona contractor—and within weeks not only was the contractor out of financial danger, but the world had another major UFO story (the case went on to win a national newspaper prize for the 'best case of 1975,' and the contractor received a cash prize from the weekly tabloid).

The central support of the Hill case is that both people told the same reports separately, and that hypnosis is a valid way to extract the truth from people who may even have forgotten it consciously. Such is the theory expounded by the pro-UFO camp regarding the Hill UFO story.

Unfortunately for them, the psychiatrist who did the original hypnosis totally disagrees. Dr. Benjamin Simon of Boston had spent hundreds of hours with Betty and Barney Hill, and had figured prominently in the book and the movie. Bound by what he saw as professional ethics, however, he did not feel at liberty to publicize his own opinions until the NBC movie made the whole case public knowledge. At last, reluctantly, he spoke out.

In Simon's professional opinion, the whole case is based on fear-induced fantasies in Betty Hill's mind. As she suffered nightmares about the original sighting (nightmares fed by hysterical UFO horror stories told her by her sister, or read in pulp science fiction monthlies), she told her friends and Barney about the dreams. It was that information which Barney was able to recall under hypnosis. Simon also pointed out that such fantasies are extremely common under hypnosis and are recognized as such by professionals, although not by editors and script writers seeking drama rather than accuracy.

What could have caused the original UFO sighting which so frightened Mrs. Hill? A young UFO investigator named Robert Sheaffer, a colleague of Klass, tried to find out. A check on astronomical and meteorological records compared to Betty Hill's testimony revealed a possible answer.

Laymen do not appreciate how often a light in the sky is misperceived as a UFO, or how often people report that their car or plane was 'chased' by a UFO which later turned out to have been a particularly bright celestial object. But even UFO believers reluctantly face up to this unfortunate type of common false alarm.

Sheaffer showed that Betty Hill's UFO was probably the bright planet Jupiter peeping out from behind a cloud, unexpectedly. The Hills, fatigued on their night journey, fell victim to an extremely common illusion, an illusion which for all its unreality can elicit real fear and terror in the people being 'chased.'

As the story was told and retold, details were added freely. Sheaffer discovered that a story 'radar confirmation' had been first mentioned by a reporter who subsequently 'lost his notes' and could not provide any proof of his claim. Other apparently corroborative details also melted away under Sheaffer's no-nonsense probe.

What about the famous star map of Zeta Reticuli? Sheaffer, an astronomer by education, pointed out that Hill only drew a collection of circles and lines which seemed pretty much at random. When an Ohio schoolteacher later spent hundreds of hours working with bead models of nearby stars, she eventually found what appeared to be a match (if stars were added or omitted to make the match work). But several other different interpretations and star identifications have also been made, and it's clear that of all the possible interpretations, no more than one can be the correct one—the others are wrong. What the different interpretations suggest (and this was mathematically demonstrated by astronomer Donald Menzel) is that any random set of dots and lines can be matched to the randomly strewn stars in the solar 'neighborhood' out to twenty or thirty light years.

These negative findings do not appear in NBC's science fiction movie which pretended it wasn't a science fiction movie. Instead, every appearance was given of a case 'based on facts.'

Probably among the millions of Americans who watched (and were misled) by the pseudo-documentary were some Arizona woodsmen who were in a tight financial bind. Team leader Mike Rogers was about to default on an already once-extended National Forestry Service contract to clear underbrush from the Apache-Sitgreaves National Forest near Snowflake. Two brothers, Travis and Duane Walton, were longtime UFO buffs who had often talked about trying to go for a ride on a flying saucer. Travis was working for Rogers, and Duane appeared later to tell newsmen about the flying saucer which had followed him around the woods one day a few years before.

Rogers had this problem: until the contract was closed out completely, or cancelled at no fault, the government withheld a portion of the payment for the acreage cleared. (An inspector determined how much had been done every week or two.) Rogers had actually been working his small crew on another, more lucrative contract (he had grossly underbid the cost of the Apache-Sitgreaves work, and now was stuck with the contracted amount), but by early November 1975, he faced a government deadline without the slightest chance of completing the work, or of getting paid the withheld amount (which could go to whomever took over the contract, so that Rogers might never receive it).

An excuse was needed to break the contract at no fault to Rogers. Of course it is impossible to say for sure what ideas the UFO movie gave the woodcutters, but the subsequent events are on record (including some events which the men tried desperately to conceal). Travis Walton vanished following a terrifying UFO sighting; the stunned woodcutters refused to return to the scene; the local Forestry officials, recognizing the superstitious fear of the locals, understandingly released Rogers from his contract and moved to pay him off. A new contractor was selected (who, by the way, had no trouble at all finding men to work in the 'haunted' forest).

As the UFO story spread across the country, UFO buffs descended on the scene. But how could the testimony of these witnesses be verified? Enter the polygraph tests, the coverups, and the scandals.

Teamed up with a weekly tabloid newspaper, one national UFO group sponsored a polygraph test for Travis Walton a few days after he had 'returned' from his UFO 'trip.' Without any physical evidence, there was nothing else to go on. One UFO group had accused Walton of being on a 'drug trip' instead, and had already pulled out of the case.

Walton flunked the polygraph test badly. The examiner reported that he had detected attempts at 'gross deception' on the part of Travis. He concluded that Walton was lying.

The stunned UFO investigators backpedaled fiercely, and quickly decided that Walton had been too overwrought to give a valid test result. They swore the investigator to secrecy and went on to proclaim that Walton had passed all tests given him. Months later, after checking out another less experienced polygraph operator with a test run on Travis's brother Duane (in which Duane 'passed' on answers which have been documented as prevarications), the UFO buffs ran Travis through—and he passed. The results were triumphantly trumpeted across the country.

There it would have rested, but one investigator was unsatisfied. Klass, who is a senior editor of a major aerospace magazine in Washington, felt that the case was shaky, so he started snooping around. He found out about the hushed up polygraph failure; he found out about the forestry contract deadline; he found out about earlier criminal records and drug activities by Travis, activities which by themselves do not disqualify him as a witness, but activities which were success- fully denied on the second polygraph round (those results were later disclaimed by the president of the polygraph firm, at about the same time as the examiner who gave them quit to become a security manager for a chain of convenience stores).

The cases of the Hills and of Walton highlight the uses of 'truth techniques' such as hypnosis and polygraphs. But these techniques have some problems in their application to the UFO field.

Take hypnotic regression, for example. Although UFO

experts used to claim that it is a sure way to extract truth from witnesses, in fact, as numerous professional psychiatrists and hypnotists have testified, the technique is subject to extremes of misinterpretation and distortion. Results can be grossly misleading as many leading UFO proponents have now admitted this publicly.

Two examples will illustrate this. A war veteran undergoing psychoanalysis had an extreme fear of fire, so with his doctor's permission he was hypnotically regressed to his wartime experiences. Under hypnosis, the soldier relived a terrifying experience in which he had been trapped inside a burning tank. Reliving this terror, he screamed and writhed in anguish, spilling forth a torrent of details about the smells, sounds, and sights of this nearly fatal experience. Somehow he escaped from the tank but was emotionally scarred for life.

The psychiatrist dug into the soldier's records for details of this terrifying incident. He was flabbergasted to discover that the man had never been in combat, and had never experienced the incident he so vividly had recreated. Instead, psychiatrists had been worried by his *excessive fears of being trapped inside a burning tank* and had pulled him off combat status.

His hypnotic story of being trapped had *never happened.* He had only imagined it happening, had feared it happening, subconsciously, for years.

In a more recent case, police in Houston have been trying to use hypnotic regression to elicit forgotten details from witnesses. In one case, two witnesses were hypnotized and asked to remember a license number of a getaway car. They both produced a number which the police attempted without success to track down. Only after weeks of frustration did a policeman notice that the number given by the witnesses was not a license number at all, but was the call number of the police officer who had first visited them, and the number had been printed prominently on the business cards he had left with them.

Such suggestibility, and the often confusing way facts can be transformed under hypnosis, is why professional hypnotists remain highly skeptical of UFO stories extracted under hypnosis. A particularly bad example of this is the famous 1976 "Kentucky abduction" of three women, investigated by several top UFO teams. The women, under hypnosis, could recall nothing about any 'occupants.' But while still under hypnotic susceptability, one of the women *was shown drawings of UFO aliens.* She soon "recalled" that indeed she, too, had seen similar beings inside the UFO. The investigators were overjoyed that the 'block had been broken.' More responsible investigators groaned in anguish when they saw how the well meaning but clumsy investigators had hopelessly contaminated the subconscious memories of the witnesses.

This brings us to the second problem with hypnosis. Recently, in California, a researcher put a dozen volunteers under hypnotic regression and asked them to retell their UFO abduction experiences. They gave long accounts filled with details on being sucked up into the ship, of the cold, the instruments, the faces of the aliens, of their questions and advice. By now, these are dismayingly run-of-the-mill stories, indistinguishable from dozens of other top UFO abduction "close encounter of the third kind" stories.

But *none of the stories were authentic.* None of the student volunteers had ever seen a UFO or had ever shown any particular interest in UFOs. None had even heard of other 'close encounters' stories. Yet when asked to recount their 'kidnapping' by 'UFO aliens,' they all had obligingly conjured up fantasies from some psychic reservoir in their imaginations. These completely baseless stories look just the same as the best UFO kidnapping stories celebrated in books, movies, and UFO pulp magazines!

What has happened? The 'close encounters' stories still could be true. But in a room full of smoke, which we thought also contained material objects, we have grasped at the clouds and have found only air in our fingers. In a body of "close encounters of the third kind" stories, we have more closely examined them and have found that they remain unconvincing—but still tantalizing.

The witnesses have *not* generally been shown to have been liars and hallucinators, so if you want to go on believing their stories, they cannot be *disproved.*

But the reliability of the stories has been seriously brought into doubt. If you wish to disbelieve in the stories, you have plenty of grounds for doing so. It is not as exciting, but it may be closer to grim and dull reality.

Yet the appeal of 'close encounter' stories continues. Why are these stories told? Why are they read with such devotion by UFO fans? That is a topic which needs study. There will always be plenty of new stories to study, that's for sure! And maybe someday one of the stories will be utterly convincing. Humans and aliens will meet, for real, and everything which came before will be forgotten. CONTACT!

Chapter Three
The Apollo 11 UFO Incidents

The epochal flight of Apollo XI to the moon occurred more than a decade ago—long enough for it to have become enshrined in our history books and our mythologies. It marked man's first landing on another world in space. It symbolized the capabilities of 20th Century American technology and management.

For the world of UFO researchers, enthusiasts and opponents, the flight of Apollo XI was also important. It became the center of a vast body of reports of alien encounters on this epic space voyage. Over the years, literally dozens of stories have been written about purported UFO sightings and photographs made during that particular mission in July 1969.

Most prestigious of the stories is the note in *Edge of Reality*, in which Dr. J. Allen Hynek, the 'dean of UFOlogy,' passes on the report that "This was the mission on which a UFO reportedly chased that spacecraft." A colleague remarked to Hynek that "during Apollo 11, Neil Armstrong, Edwin Aldrin, and Michael Collins said they observed a UFO." Hynek agreed, and elaborated: "Some of the NASA movie frames that I examined were most interesting—particularly those taken on the Apollo 11 flight, one of the few for which NASA has not come up with some sort of explanation."

In *Science Digest*, the respected monthly popular science journal, astronomer-author James Mullaney (a former contributing editor to *Astronomy* magazine) wrote in July 1977 that "the crew of Apollo 11, during the first moon landing, reporting that their capsule was paced by what appeared to be a mass of intelligent energy....NASA recently released a number of very striking Gemini, Apollo, and Skylab photos of true unidentifieds."

The UFO press has widely reported such stories, both in books, movies, and magazines.

UFOs Past, Present and Future (written by Robert Emenegger, researched by Alan Frank Sandler) reported on "perhaps the most spectacular of all sightings" which occurred on Apollo 11. On the way out to the moon, the astronauts watched an object which seemed to change shape when they switched magnifications of their telescope. "It was really weird," Collins is quoted as saying.

Fate magazine, in editor Curtis Fuller's column "I See By The Papers" (November 1970), examined the stories and concluded: "There seems to be pretty good evidence that Buzz Aldrin, Neil Armstrong, and Michael Collins saw something that hasn't been made generally known—something variously reported, ranging from mysterious lights to formations of spaceships!"

The authenticity of the Apollo 11 sightings has been vouched for by testimony attributed to CBS TV news anchorman Walter Cronkite. In an interview with the *National Enquirer*, conducted by reporter Robin Leach, Cronkite gave this account: "En route for the world's first moon landing, Armstrong and the crew transmitted some earthshaking information. And I was there to hear it for myself."

Cronkite continued: "Armstrong claimed to have spotted a huge cylindrical object which was rotating or tumbling between the ship and the moon. It's officially recorded in the NASA record vaults that Armstrong indicated he went to take photographs but the object vanished as quickly as he'd first seen it. Neil Armstrong is not a man given to fanciful imagination and it wasn't just one of the crew that saw it—they all did, and you have to respect those men."

That was good enough for *Ripley's Believe It or Not*, too. In late 1978 they published a syndicated series of cartoon panels dealing with UFOs; one panel contained a sketch of astronauts and the caption, "Astronaut Neil Armstrong...saw UFOs while on space mission. But NASA—according to newcaster Walter Cronkite—is keeping the evidence a secret."

But the secret leaked a little, according to the McGraw-Hill Publishing Company. In 1979 they issued a book by David C. Knight, entitled *UFOs: A Pictorial History*. A full-page space photo on page 171 bears this caption: "Perhaps the most spectacular of all UFO sightings from space occurred on July 19, 1969 on the Apollo-11 flight. . . . The crew spotted a strange object between their ship and the moon. . . . The object still remains unidentified." (Purists might have noted that the object shown on the page was between the ship and the *earth*, but who wants to be picky when dealing with such fantastic stories?).

An idea of what these secrets might entail can be obtained from a summary of the circulated Apollo 11 stories published by Mike Harris in a New Zealand UFO newsletter in 1974:

From the launching of Apollo 11 on July 16th, 1969, until the spacecraft passed the midpoint between the earth and the moon the following day, the three astronauts observed a U.F.O. keeping pace with them. Two days later, on July 19th at approximately 1800 hours, U.F.O.s made another appearance and were recorded on film. The details of this extensive film were: the day before the lunar landing Aldrin transferred to the L. M. "Eagle" and began the final instrument checks. Whilst checking the close-up camera, the U.F.O.s came into the picture. Whilst under observation, the objects were seen to be emitting what looked like some kind of liquid. The two objects were in close formation and would come together and part and after some time separated and went off their own ways. The objects appeared to be intelligently controlled, the astronauts said. The third sighting during this epic flight occurred on July 21st, 00.26 hours. About an hour and a half previously, Neil Armstrong and Aldrin had set foot on the moon. While they were busy gathering rocks, Collins in the Command Module 'Columbia' was busy talking to Houston.

Columbia: Calling Houston. This is Columbia.

Houston: Go ahead, Columbia.

Columbia: I couldn't find the L. M. But I saw some weird small white objects. Co-ordinates are 0.3, 7.6 on the southwest edge of the crater. If they're there they should have seen them too.

It seems likely that whoever was interested in our efforts was certainly keeping an eye on things. The report goes on:

These white objects seen by Collins made a fourth appearance as the "Eagle" was rising from the Lunar Surface to re-unite with the "Columbia," having left the moon at 13.55 on July 21st. Their shape in this case was clearly exposed on film. The fixed camera on the "Eagle" was photographing the moon's receding surface when, diagonally from the lower left to the upper right of the frames, a white, shining U.F.O. passed directly under the Lunar Module.

This is certainly a sensational scenario for mankind's first landing on another world, and it is in addition a version certainly *not* described by the standard history books. Corroborating accounts come from Michael Hervey's book *UFOs The American Scene* (St. Martin's Press, NY, 1976). In lunar orbit, Aldrin is adjusting his camera when suddenly:

> ...his attention was suddenly drawn to a bright object resembling a "snowman" travelling from west to east in the sky. He immediately took some shots of the object which in fact proved to be two UFOs, one larger than the other, and almost touching. When the film was developed later it included a shot of the moon's surface to be followed by a close-up of the two UFOs moving at a high speed horizontally. They disappeared, only to return a few seconds later, descended a little, hovered for a while, and then separated, whereupon they were surrounded by "what looked like a strong halation." They followed this manoeuvre by rising vertically and disappearing from sight. In due course only one UFO returned, and then again took its leave for the last time. Astronauts Armstrong and Aldrin were naturally excited and perhaps a little apprehensive during those few moments.

Yet for all the drama of this event, none of it seems to have been disclosed by the NASA public affairs officers in Houston. Clearly, some sort of coverup was involved. The first major break in this apparent coverup did not occur until 1974, when the Cosmic Brotherhood Association, a Japanese UFO group published hitherto unavailable photos from Apollo 11 with this comment:

> The pictures of UFOs taken by Apollo 11 spaceship over the moon's surface for the first time in the world and now published by CBA (Cosmic Brotherhood Association) for the first time, cannot but be considered the firm evidence that UFOs, so far questioned by many, are actually spaceship/spacecraft come from outer space as we have been asserting. They are the absolute evidence sought by the world's UFOlogists for the past 27 years....Following are overwhelming proof of UFOs, they came from outer space ....They are really scoop pictures, and not even one of them has been released by NASA as yet.

This sensational news crossed the Pacific and was noted by

UFO expert Bob Barry of the "Twentieth Century UFO Bureau," who wrote up a two part survey of astronaut UFO experiences for *Modern People,* a weekly tabloid newspaper. The UFO article was later combined with other similar material which was published in magazine form as *UFO Report* (issued in 1975, only one issue ever came out). "NASA Hiding UFOs From You!" screamed the headline:

> En route to the Moon on their first day in space, the crew of Columbia sighted a strange object hovoring high above the earth, and managed to capture it on film. NASA's photo interpretation lab listed the object as unidentifiable. But this was only the beginning. Before this mission would come to an end, the crew of Columbia and later the Eagle, would see a lot more UFO action—over the moon itself!

Barry then describes the encounter of Aldrin with the two UFOs zooming across his window in lunar orbit. Luckily, says Barry, Aldrin was used to seeing UFOs in space, so he could do the right thing quickly:

> If Aldrin had not been somewhat conditioned to the appearance of these unusual craft, the shock of what he saw next might have caused him to miss one of the most amazing sequences of film taken of UFOs by any astronaut. For as the objects continued their descent in a formation similar to that of a "snowman" laid on its side, Aldrin observed a brilliant emission extending from between the two craft. Speculation at the time was that this "trail" was possibly connected to the vehicles' motivational systems, possibly even an exhaust....During this time, ten other egg-shaped objects were seen flying in the foreground of the camera's view. Naturally, NASA did not release these photos to the general public, taking great pains to edit any such mysterious craft from the final stills which were released....And even though almost every crew that has traveled to the moon has witnessed and photographed unidentified flying objects, NASA officials still insist that such phenomena do not exist.

But even Barry's spectacular photographic evidence is not the most exciting report to come out of the flight of Apollo 11. For only shortly after this astronauts returned to earth in mid-1969, a bootleg "tape" and voice transcript of what was *really* said on the moon has been circulating clandestinely in UFO circles. The headline on the cover of *National Bulletin* magazine (distributed in Canada but printed in New York City) for September 29, 1969, cries out that "Phony Transmission Failure Hides Apollo 11

Discovery....Moon is a U.F.O. Base!" Author Sam Pepper gave this version of the "Top Secret Tape Transcript" from "a leak close to the top," as follows:

What was it, what the hell was it? That's all I want to know....

These...(garbled)...babies were huge, sir, they were enormous....

No, No, that's just field distortion....

Oh, God, you wouldn't believe it....

What...what...what the hell's going on? Whatsa matter with you guys...?

They're here, under the surface....

What's there...malfunction...Mission Control calling Apollo 11....

Roger, we're here, all three of us, but we've found some visitors....

Yeah, they've been here for quite a while judging by the installations....

Mission control, repeat last message....

I'm telling you, there are other spacecraft out there. They're lined up in ranks on the far side of the crater edge....

Repeat, repeat....

Let's get that orbit scanned and head home....

In 625 to the fifth, auto-relays set...My hands are shaking so bad....

Film...yes, the damned cameras were clicking away from up here...

Did you fellows get anything?

Had no film left by the time...(garbled)...three shots of the saucers, or whatever they were...may have fogged the film.

Mission Control, this is Mission Control...are you under way, repeat, are you under way? What's this uproar about UFOs? Over.

They're set up down there...they're on the moon... watching us....

The mirrors, the mirrors...you set them up, didn't you?

Yes, the mirrors are all in place. But whatever built those spacecraft will probably come over and pull 'em all out by the roots tomorrow....

When this account was discussed by *Fate* editor Curtis Fuller in 1970, he confessed to "extreme skepticism about the whole alleged transcription." But the account has been printed elsewhere, (science fiction author and UFO buff Otto Binder helped spread it widely), and it reminds observers of the radio signals picked up in Europe in the early 1960s from doomed Russian cosmonauts on secret space shots which ended in their undisclosed deaths. Radio amateurs have become very proficient in smoking out 'official secrets' in the past few decades.

Nor do these eye-opening (and hair-raising?) stories end here. Another "inside account" appeared in the monthly bulletin of the well-known UFO group, APRO (Aerial Phenomena Research Organization). As reported in the February 1976 issue, three disc-shaped shadows paced the astronauts as they circled the moon, while NASA censors cut off further live comments from the newsmen. An APRO informant known as "Mister X" was allegedly present in the "inner control room."

The astronauts, recalled the otherwise unidentified "Mister X," suddenly said, "There they are again," referring to objects spotted on the first three orbits and the last orbit. It seems to be an independent corroboration of stories recounted earlier.

Additionally, a new and hitherto unavailable Apollo 11 photograph was published in the monthly *Science Digest* in the issue immediately following that which contained Mullaney's article. Discussing Project Bluebook, author Don Berliner's article includes a photograph showing the earth receding from the moonship, and a UFO right smack dab in the middle. Says *Science Digest* (Aug. 1977), "Arrow points toward an unidentified object."

As might be expected, NASA officially denies it all. No extraordinary UFOs or other unexplained phenomena have been admitted.

When the "Pepper Transcript" first became public, UFO buffs wrote to their congressmen demanding that NASA officially confess to the coverup. NASA replied that "the incidents... did not take place. Conversations between the Apollo 11 crew and Mission Control were released live during the entire Apollo 11 mission. There were between 1000 and 1500 representatives of the news media and TV present at the Houston News Center listening and observing, and not one has suggested that NASA withheld any news or conversations of this nature." (Letter from Assistant Administrator for Legislative Affairs to several congressmen, January 1970).

In 1976, Chief of the Astronaut Office Deke Slayton claimed that "I don't recall any of our astronauts ever reporting UFOs."

NASA claims that all photos, all voice transcripts, all debriefings are in the public domain and are available to the news media. This data is too voluminous to publish openly, but is

Outbound from Earth, the spaceship was surrounded by a blizzard of tiny, tumbling particles shaken loose when the Lunar module was pulled free of its S-4-B booster "garage." One particle appeared in one of a series of tourist shots of the receding Earth.

But in a UFO article in *Science Digest* in 1977, the particle is airbrushed out and a spurious "UFO" is inexplicably present. Editor Dan Button insisted his version was the original and NASA was censoring other editions of the photograph.

available to researchers with appropriate credentials in Houston, Flagstaff, and Washington. And as a matter of fact, no researcher (UFO or otherwise) has ever filed a complaint that data was witheld from him when he tried to get it. (Although Barry and Sandler *have* made vague allegations).

The photographic documentation, including film magazine inventories, exposure logs, and control documents, have been examined by researchers. All the film is accounted for. Evidently, NASA is quite correct in saying that everything is available....

...But to whom? Almost 1500 still photos and dozens of magazines of film were exposed on Apollo 11. Transcripts run to the thousands of pages. Who has taken the trouble to check out all this material?

I have, for example. Other writers have. Also, Dr. J. Allen Hynek visited the Houston space center in July 1976 and was shown the material in question. NASA's original story, surprisingly, has been confirmed: All the material is available. He said as much in a *Playboy* interview in January 1978, but his book still carries the phony list and there is no indication it has been removed from later editions. Hynek's opinion: these UFO stories are *false*.

Fuller's skepticism about the "Pepper Transcript" appears to have been justified. From internal evidence alone, it looks more and more like a crude hoax. This can be deduced from the vocabulary itself:

"Mission Control"...this was *never* a phrase used by astronauts, who instead referred always to "Houston."

Technical-sounding gibberish such as "field distortion," "orbit scanned," "625 to the fifth," "auto-relays," etc. were never found in real transcripts.

"Repeat, repeat" is never used on the radio; instead, astronauts and Mission Control use the phrase "Say Again."

"Three of us"...actually, only two men were on the lunar surface.

In addition, interviews with the handful of amateur radio listeners who are known to have tuned in the S-Band (2270 megahertz) moon signals produced testimony that they heard the same conversations which were released by NASA. Since listening to the moon required the use of ten-foot diameter radio dishes, few people actually could do it, and they were known to each other, having done similar space eavesdropping for years.

(The consensus among such experienced American "hams" is that the old stories of "radio transmissions from secret dying Russian spacemen" were either dumb mistakes, outright hoaxes, or playful publicity stunts by Italian and German radio amateurs.)

The unavoidable conclusion is that Pepper either fabricated the fake "transcript" himself or used very poor judgement in allowing himself to be victimized by somebody else's fake. As is often the case with UFO reports, it is very hard to prove definitely that something did *not* happen. But in this case, fortunately, the hoax was so rickety that it collapses under its own weight.

More puzzling is Collins' report about the "weird white objects" which the Japanese sources said had been spotted near the Lunar Module. These could have been the same UFOs reported in the Pepper transcript.

But they weren't, because here is what Collins really said to Houston on that orbit: "I did see a suspiciously small white object whose coordinates are Easy 0.3, 7.6, right on the southwest end of a crater, but I think they would know it if they were in such a location. It looks like their LM would be pitched up quite a degree. It's on the southwest wall of a smallish crater." (Tape 71/16 page 396).

So Collins is trying to spot the LM from a hundred miles overhead, but he cannot; instead he sees *one* white object (a rock?) on the edge of a crater. He doubts it is the LM because if it were, the LM would be highly tilted and the astronauts there would have noticed the *tilt*—which they didn't. Collins did *not* spot a fleet of UFOs, as the very loose rewording of this account might lead someone to suspect. Compare the words to the UFO rewording—is it just sloppy, or is it a deliberate distortion?

These are details. How about the key sighting, the "snowman," and Aldrin's movie film? What could possibly explain that?

All that is needed to explain it is for anybody to view the film. The scenes in question come from "Magazine F" ('Foxtrot'), on the first twenty-five feet or so, and can (as can all other Apollo 11 flight film) be purchased from the National Audiovisual Company, 1411 South Fern Street, Arlington, Virginia 22202.

The actual film shows a window full of dazzling, dancing, dizzying *reflections* and *glares*. Viewing the film in motion, there can be no question of the lights being solid objects outside the spaceship. There is no way I could imagine that a viewer could *honestly* believe that UFOs were being shown. The "emissions" are just more fuzzy reflections.

Examination of a few stills from that filmstrip shows what happened to the original appearance of the "UFOs." The Japanese UFO group touched up the photos, enhancing the contrast of the lights, and cropping out the extraneous reflections. Further, the

This is the camera, and the window mount in the lunar module, which took the magazine-F "UFO films." Photograph courtesy of NASA

films were airbrushed to downplay any additional reflections which might remain, aside from the two globes of light. They became the supposed UFOs which, needless to say, the crew didn't see. (The film, by the way, was taken from orbit the day before the landing—*not* from the surface.)

These UFO photos, in other words, are a *fraud*, plain and simple. They are part of a space forgery haox gone wild and run out of control. There never were any such "snowmen" UFOs as claimed.

But UFO expert Michael Hervey had written that the astronauts had actually used the words "snowman" and "halation," and that they were naturally excited and perhaps a little apprehensive. UFO expert Matsumura in Japan gave numerous details of Aldrin's actual movements during the encounter. UFO expert Bob Barry wrote that Aldrin observed the UFOs directly, and that the astronauts speculated about the mystery emission.

On July 19, 1969, the day before historic Moon landing, astronaut Edwin Aldrin Jr. took this exclusive picture of the lunar surface—complete with UFOs.

NASA Hiding UFOs From You

The most sensational Apollo-11 UFO was the "snowman" reportedly seen and photographed by Edwin "Buzz" Aldrin.

None of these things seems to have happened. The writers were dramatizing the event based on the forged photographs. Less sympathetic critics would suggest that the authors were fictionalizing the event, or even less charitably, were lying.

"That's a bunch of baloney," Barry retorted when he heard these charges in 1978. "They can deny all they want, we have the proof."

But it will take more than Barry's bravado to stare down the actual proof of Apollo 11 "Magazine Foxtrot." The movies do not lie; they show the dancing lights, the reflections, the glare. They do not show *any* UFOs.

Nor will *Science Digest* soon live down its double-barreled UFO flop. First, Mullaney's claim about the Apollo 11 crew reporting a mass of intelligent energy is clearly a further elaboration of the original Matsumura-CBA forgery, without any effort to check out the story with NASA. Second, the photograph published in *Science Digest* the following month was also retouched: Editor Dan Button admitted that certain extraneous pieces of space debris were airbrushed out to avoid detracting from the true UFO, but all previously published and released versions of that same photograph show absolutely empty space where *Science Digest* points to an "unidentified object." Either somebody got a bad print with an extra spot on the negative, or somebody at the Hearst Corporation monthly added the "UFO" into the photo for dramatic effect. Button accuses NASA of another coverup; informed observers can now judge whose dishonesty Button is trying to cover up.

Actually, one Apollo 11 photo *does* show a true unidentified (but hardly unidentifiable) object. Soon after pulling the LM out of the rocket garage, near the earth, a flood of spinning particles rushed past the Apollo's windows. One of the astronauts was taking a series of tourist snapshots of the receding earth, and in one of the photos was a tiny odd-shaped blob.

There is no indication that any of the astronauts saw it. Since it's out of focus on a camera with an extremely wide depth of field, photographic experts have concluded that it was probably only a few feet outside the window, and an inch or two across. As on other flights, pieces of insulation and ice surrounded the Apollo at this stage in the flight. "Unidentified" it certainly might be, but it could not by any semantic word game be called an authentic UFO—except, for example, in McGraw-Hill's *UFOs a Pictorial History!*

The crew did indeed report to earth about another tiny object they watched through their monocular. To some of the astronauts, it looked cylindrical, just like their spent rocket stage which was known to be pacing them in a parallel orbit. Said Armstrong, "It was right at the limit of resolution of the eye; it was very difficult to tell just what shape it was." NASA's reasonable assumption was that it was indeed the rocket stage, since it was behaving just like a rocket stage should; other Apollo flights had reported much the same thing.

The entire Cronkite interview in the *National Enquirer* was a fake, evidently assembled by a free lance writer. The newspaper refused to take the blame when Cronkite complained—but fired the writer.

And what can one say about "Mister X" report? Again, from the internal evidence of the details "X" gives in an attempt to establish credibility with listeners, space experts have quickly figured out that he never could have been near the real Mission Control Center—his jargon is so mixed up. In other words, they concluded this is just another tall tale. Claims that these voice signals were cut off from the newsmen who were present are also in complete contradiction with personal accounts of newsmen who were in Houston: There was no significant tape delay, and there were no silences indicative of censorship.

But the stories crossed the Atlantic into a French UFO book, and then came back home reinforced and newly authenticated in Maurice Chatelain's *Our Ancestors Came From Outer Space* (Doubleday, 1978).* According to the author, who claimed to be an ex-NASA space scientist (actually, he had worked for a space contractor in Los Angeles for several years): "The astronauts... saw things during their missions that could not be discussed with anybody outside NASA. It is very difficult to obtain any specific information from NASA, which still exercises a very strict control over any disclosures of these events...It seems that all Apollo and Gemini flights were followed...by space vehicles of extraterrestrial origin...Every time it occurred, the astronauts informed Mission Control, who then ordered absolute silence...."

Chatelain specifically mentions Apollo-11, which "made the first moon landing on the Sea of Tranquillity and, only moments before Armstrong stepped down the ladder to set foot on the moon, two UFOs hovered overhead. Edwin Aldrin took several pictures of them...."

Even more sensational was the claim for the Apollo-13 flight: "There was some talk that the Apollo 13 mission carried a nuclear device aboard that could be set off to make measurements of the infrastructure of the moon and whose detonations would show on the charts of several recording seismographs placed in different locations. The unexplained explosion of an oxygen tank in the service module of Apollo 13 on its flight to the moon, according to rumors, was caused deliberately by a UFO that was following the capsule to prevent the (nuclear) detonation...."

Of course, the cause of the explosion was found by NASA later, and there was no nuclear device—rumors of UFO attacks are absurd. But that's no reason for some UFO people not to pass on and embellish such stories, as we'll see.

The Russian UFO enthusiasts were next in line on this cosmic relay race. The July 1978 issue of The *UFO Journal,* published by the Mutual UFO Network, highlighted a speech made in Russia on November 24, 1977, by Vladimir G. Azhazha. Speaking to a group of NOVOSTI news service employees, at the Academy of Sciences in Moscow, Azhazha related that: "The

---

*A French edition appeared first in 1976.

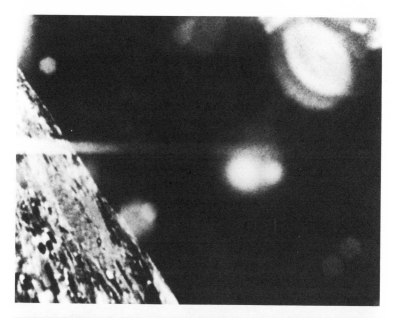

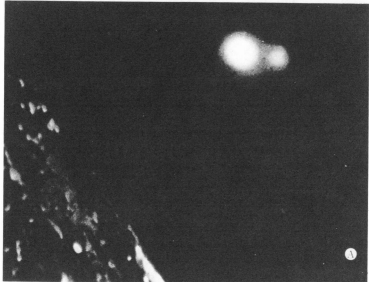

American astronauts who visited the moon saw a gigantic cylinder 1500 meters (about one mile) long there. Aldrin shot it on movie film. The vehicle accomplished its own interactions with Apollo; it coordinated its movement with it. . . .

"The. . .reports of the American astronauts who visited the

moon are exceptionally interesting. Their agreed-upon code for designating UFOs was the phrase 'Saint Nicholas,' but, they were so amazed with what they saw when they arrived on the moon from Apollo that they transmitted to Earth without the code: 'Directly across from us, on the other side of the crater, there are other spaceships observing us.' And Aldrin shot his film which shows the UFOs on the moon...."

Azhazha discloses that his source of this data is the book by Chatelain, continuing that "The moon is evidently a transhipment base for UFOs and every Apollo which has flown to the moon has been under the 'observation' canopy of the UFOs. It was not by accident that the American astronauts were not successful in their attempt to explode a nuclear device for scientific purposes on the moon. Instead, the oxygen cylinder on Apollo exploded. They were also not able to blow up the upper stage of the booster and so it continues to fly around the moon...." Presumably with a UFO escort.

MUFON director Walt Andrus noted in the preface to this article that "...a Washington DC news source...has informed me that the statements attributed to astronaut Buzz Aldrin about the UFOs on the moon were confirmed by his bureau's space reporter, who covered the Apollo story at the time. *Aldrin said them as a joke.* It is possible that the story filtered through to the Soviet Union in garbled form, as is evident in some other cases...Other portions of this report still may be significant...."

Andrus, in other words, considered it sufficient to ask a friend to ask a friend to dredge up ten-year-old memories—and he called it 'research.' Andrus continued: "The previously unpublished Russian document...speaks of sensational events and high-level government knowledge that have been withheld from the public. The alleged events need to be authenticated, for, if true, they are of profound importance. Astronaut movie films of UFOs on the moon?...There is a clear need to learn how much of all this 'sensationalism' is actually true, and to expose as false all that is false." These brave words, from a man considered to be one of the more rational and reliable UFO experts, are not matched by Andrus's actions or, apparently, his intentions to publish any exposé. The astronaut UFO stories are too "useful" to risk examining them very closely.

So widespread is the Russian UFO enthusiasm that official government denials have become necessary. In the November 1978 issue of *Culture and Life* (published in Moscow) Soviet astronomer Vladimir Krat is asked to refute such stories as:

Interviewer: They say that the American astronauts

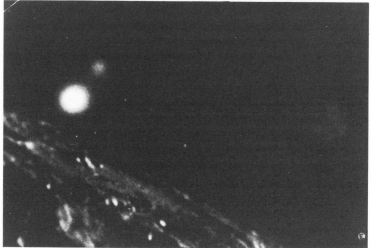

who had landed on the Moon had to make a small explosion in order to cause an artificial moonquake, but that they failed to do this. A mysterious blast on board the ship broke an oxygen cylinder. It might have been caused by a flying saucer observing the ship, so as to stop an experiment which could have destroyed bases set up by extra-terrestrial civilizations on the Moon. "What's this? What's the matter, damn it? I should like to know the truth, what is it? There are other spaceships here!" Armstrong is alleged to have shouted upon seeing several UFOs on the other side of a crater. But Aldrin saw at once what the matter was and started communicating with the Earth in a secret code. Later, all information about the incident was made secret by the Americans. There is talk about other cases of cosmonauts seeing UFOs. Special emphasis is laid on the fact that the first four or five hours of one of the crews' stay on the Moon remain a mystery—what the astronauts did during that time has not been made public.

Krat: The astronauts' flights to the Moon were followed by all mankind, their work on the surface of the Moon is known down to the minute. I see no logic in the talk about any information being instantly made "classified." Why should the Americans have made a secret out of their meeting some creatures from other planets, had any such a rendezvous taken place at all? Would they have been afraid to cause panic on Earth? But there were no special grounds for panic."

Clearly, Krat is unaware of the scope of the distortions in such stories and can only come up with bland disclaimers which would convince nobody.

What Krat should have done was to examine the hearsay more closely. The "mysterious blast" was the explosion on Apollo 13, which has been attributed to hostile UFO action. The "artificial moonquakes" on *later* flights worked quite well, although Chatelain and Azhazha claim that *nuclear* explosives were to have been used! The "secret code" is Chatelain's idea: he claims that the astronauts used the phrase "Santa Claus" to refer to UFOs. As for the missing "four or five hours," I drew a blank; so I suspect the Russian just made it up.

As expected, the phony Apollo 11 UFO stories continue to be recirculated and embellished. In June 1979 a Dell paperback entitled *Secrets of Our Spaceship Moon* by Detroit schoolteacher Don Wilson, appeared on the newsstands. Its front cover screams: "THE NASA COVERUP—Here are the facts they couldn't hide! What did the men on the moon really see?" The front inside page blurb proclaims, "here at last is the complete uncensored story: clear and indisputable facts offered by astronomers and the astronauts themselves, despite NASAs' continued official denials...."

The Apollo 11 sightings provide only a portion of the arguments in the book, but they are highlighted. Bob Barry's

'snowman UFO' is featured, with Wilson's claim that "Buzz
Aldrin ground away with his camera, taking invaluable (but now
secret) footage of the two mysterious objects." The claim that the
film shows UFOs is, as we've seen, silly; the claim that the film is
'now secret' is an outrageous falsehood.

Every other reputed Apollo 11 UFO encounter is faithfully
and unquestioningly reproduced by Wilson, although he does
point out in some cases that they are 'unauthenticated.' Equally
unauthenticated is UFO buff James Harder's claims that he found

voice tapes of UFO encounters on Apollo 11, which NASA privately admitted to him had been suppressed "for fear of public panic."

"The evidence we have cited in this book," Wilson concludes later, "proves that we have on our hands today another Watergate—a cosmic Watergate...We showed incontrovertable evidence that NASA is hiding the fact that UFOs were seen by astronauts...A study of the records and a glance at the photos will convince even the most diehard skeptic that this is exactly what happened when man went to the moon." Such bluster is not related to the actual evidence—in fact, the pattern we've seen shows that the less reliable the evidence, the more flowery the boasts and threats. Wilson blusters—but has only fake evidence. Dell paperbacks, according to editor James Frenkel, saw no reason to check up on these incredible accounts, but decided just to trust Wilson.

The Aldrin-snowman-UFO received a new champion in 1980 when another UFO expert proclaimed that the object was not a space craft but instead a space creature, or·"critter!"

Writing in *Frontiers of Science* (formerly *Second Look*, the magazine which absorbed Hynek's *International UFO Reporter* and which for tax purposes is published under the aegis of the Center for UFO Studies), paranormal specialist John White (author of *Pole Shift!* and numerous other books), claims that the space pix are identical to others taken on Earth by Trevor James Constable, a disciple of orgone energy advocate Wilhelm Reich. Constable has pushed the theory that UFOs are bizarre living (and not necessarily intelligent) creatures which inhabit the upper atmosphere and—evidently—outer space as well (in such books as *The Cosmic Pulse of Life*, Steinerbooks, 1976). Usually the "critters" (as Constable prefers to call them) are invisible and can only be captured on infra-red film.

"Even the astronauts who took pictures of UFOs in space failed to recognize the living creatures for what they are," wrote White. The snowman photo is "highly disputed—is the luminous sphere a space critter?" Acknowledging my published evaluation of the source of the images, White disagrees but admits he is "not yet in a position to disprove [(Oberg's)] contention." He also displayed in the article a copy of the outbound blob: "((It)) appears to show a large critter looming above the Earth."

White has no love lost for NASA. Earlier, in a guest editorial for Timothy Green Beckley's *UFO Review* tabloid newspaper, White has accused NASA of a nasty coverup: "Proof already exists, much of it long-known to NASA." White then refers to the *Edge of Reality* for a list of astronaut sightings (a list long repudiated by its authors, as we saw), and *Modern People* tabloid (the January 1978 issue), "for leaked NASA photographs of UFOs including *plasmatic animals* [(italics added)]." NASA spokesmen, according to White, are "either woefully ignorant of the facts....or else deliberately attempt to mislead the public. The public has more common sense in this matter than most NASA bureaucrats."

Constable, meanwhile, was delighted to endorse White's interpretation of the Apollo 11 photographs. In a 1981 issue of the irregular *Metascience Quarterly*, he crowed: "How strange it seems that NASA has recorded images just like mine . . . and *suppresses* the photos . . :. Thanks to John's enterprise, we now have a 'NASA Critter Collection,' but they are worming out of it by having loudmouth Oberg identify these photos as frauds. Pure social pathology!" Aha, social pathology indeed!

(Such *ad hominem* reaction from the crackpots is hardly unusual. In 1979, Gray Barker, a long-time fringe UFO personality and satirist, referred to me in a discussion praising Timothy Green Beckley's research: "When these exposes by Beckley and others began generating letters to Congress, NASA official Capt. James Oberg led a one-man crusade to squelch these rumors. Many people in civilian UFO research believe Capt. Oberg was specially assigned to this mission to discount these news leaks of astronaut sightings. "And one high MUFON (Mutual UFO Network, a private UFO research organization) official spread the story in the mid-1970s that *I* was Philip Klass's 'ghostwriter' in his anti-UFO books! That's right, when you don't like the testimony, smear the witness—an old crooked lawyer's trick.)

Fittingly enough, the ultimate word (too date!) in these Apollo 11 absurdities lies with the old familiar *National Enquirer*, the weekly grocery store tabloid known for its Hollywood gossip, psychic predictions, miracle medical cures, and flying saucer stories. "Aliens on Moon When We Landed" was the screaming banner headline on the September 11, 1979 issue (the same story made the September 9 *Sunday Mirror* in London and was subsequently endorsed in the backdated July-August 1979 issue of the prestigious British journal, *Flying Saucer Review*).

"The astronauts saw UFOs and even photographed them," wrote the authors (Eric Faucher, Ellen Goodstein, and Henry Gris), "but the stupifying close encounter has been kept completely under wraps by NASA until now...(they evidently hadn't read—or hadn't believed—the Cronkite interview in their own paper!). NASA's coverup was so massive that the news has taken ten years to reach the American public—and had to be first disclosed by Soviet scientists,who found out about it two years ago."

And that's the catch: the *National Enquirer*, in a man-bites-dog reversal of standard practice, had been itself a victim of somebody else's news hoax. The source was none other than Vladimir Azhazha, who somehow neglected to mention to Henry Gris, his contact, that the story was based entirely, not on official Soviet sources, but on Chatelain's strange 'ancient astronauts' book! "I am absolutely certain this episode took place," Azhazha told Gris (who is fluent in Russian) during a telephone interview. "According to our information...his (Armstrong's) message was never heard by the public—because NASA censored it."

According to Gris (who was soon thereafter discharged from the staff of the *National Enquirer*). Azhazha "refused to identify the source of his information—but he and other Russian space experts say the encounter has been common knowledge among Soviet scientific circles."

To close the loop by swallowing its own tail/tale, the *National Enquirer* then quoted from...*Maurice Chatelain*, "a former top consultant to NASA," who supposedly corroborated independently the Soviet version of the story! Also testifying were leading UFOlogists Leonard Stringfield of MUFON ("If the government released one little bit of what happened on the moon, it would be the story of the century" is how he's quoted, but he subsequently denied saying anything like that); John Schuessler ("I work with astronauts at NASA and have heard the story from them" is how he's quoted, but he has since angrily charged that Ellen Goodstein dropped the "never" which he spoke before "heard."); Timothy Green Beckley (who has privately admitted the incidents never occurred but that they are too good for publicity to criticize); Joseph Goodavage (a noted astrologer-author well known for distorting and dramatizing uncooperative facts, as we'll see in a later chapter); and "scientist Fred Bell" (who apparently is a figment of co-author Eric Faucher's imagination). So even if the *National Enquirer* was originally the victim of Azhazha's deception, it was the newspaper's staff who added their own peculiar brand of journalism, and it was the newspaper's readership who were ultimately victimized.

Even Moscow admits that! A lengthy anti-UFO article ("The Legend of the Visitors," *Pravda*, March 2, 1980, p. 6), by science correspondent Vladimir Gubarev) reported: "People have confidence in the testimony of cosmonauts and astronauts," Gubarev wrote. "So why not take them as allies, decided the UFO propagandists? Thus here in the ten years after the flights to the moon, the fantasists, who sometimes present themselves as scientific workers, claim in their public lectures that astronauts, visiting the moon, have many times observed UFOs, and that Neil Armstrong reported to Houston: Here are located large objects, sir! Enormous ones! Oh God! Here are located other space ships! They are standing along the side of the crater! They are located on the moon and they are observing us!"

Gubarev continued his article: "It's a fruitless task to search for these words in the transcripts of radio transmissions from the crew of Apollo 11, they're not there. Yes, and not a single person listening to the radio-reporting from the moon—and it went out over the air live—paid any attention to similar information— strange, isn't it true?

"At a meeting with Neil Armstrong I asked him about 'flying saucers.' "We didn't see them," answered the astronaut; "and with what we, cosmonauts and astronauts, are doing in space, that's a real wonder."

Gubarev also reported on an interview with Pete Conrad, concerning his alleged UFOs on Apollo 12 (there weren't any), and later also recounts an incident from early 1978 when the Russian crewmen of Salyut-6 were startled to see "UFOs" near their space station which turned out to be recently trash bags jettisoned. The article in *Pravada* closed with very negative conclusions about gullible people who easily fall for nonsense such as UFOs and religion! While it may be risky to believe *anything* anyone says in *Pravda* (which means 'Truth,' in Russian), the appearance of this article and others like it testifies to the official displeasure at the widespread Soviet popular enthusiasm for such tales.

Wherever there is widespread popular interest in a topic, you will find the vultures swooping in to prey on eager gullibiles and their willingness to spend money on books which boast new, lurid revelations. So it shouldn't have been much of a surprise that Charles Berlitz (author of several highly profitable "Bermuda Triangle" books) should have decided to "discover" the Apollo 11 UFO encounters in 1980. This was revealed in his latest book, *The Roswell Incident* (all the actual research seems to have been done by his co-author William Moore and by UFO advocate and former nuclear engineer Stanton Friedman), whose main theme is that the US government captured a crashed flying saucer in mid-1947, along with the dead bodies of the beings who had made up its crew, and has successfully stashed it all away since then while studying the materials.

Berlitz has nothing new to offer besides further garbling of the same old fairy tales. He bases his information on Maurice Chatelain ("based on information picked up from 'inside sources' while working for NASA in the 1960s") about "reports of these encounters made during flights in space (which) have generally been censored, altered, de-emphasized, or simply ignored by NASA." Here's the ol' Apollo 11 story a la Berlitz, 1980:

"Prior to the first moon landing two UFOs and a long cylinder hovered overhead. When Apollo 11 landed inside a moon crater two unidentified spacecrafts (sic) appeared on the crater rim and then took off again. Aldrin photographed them. Pictures have not yet been released by NASA to the public."

Mr. Berlitz's next pages reprint much of the long-discredited Pepper transcript, as well as a series of other astronaut-UFO fables. Moore later denied any endorsement of the stories merely because he put them in the book (he wanted to "set the stage" and keep an open mind), but Friedman denounced the story in 1981 and justified his cooperation with Berlitz because he needed the money and publicity in order to advance his research.

It might be interesting here to learn just what NASA public information officials think about this long series of retellings of the great moon flight UFO. To do just that, I arranged an interview early in 1980 with two highly respected space experts at the Johnson Space Center in Houston, Terry White and Charles Redmond. To convey the full flavor of the conversation, here is how it went:

Question: How do you guys find out about such UFO stories? Do the authors and publishers try to check up on them?

White: I usually first hear about them when some newsman telephones me, claiming he's seen another exposure of some "NASA coverup." The people who write such stories—they rarely have the courtesy or courage to send us pre-publication copies.

Redmond: The only time I recall ever being asked for an explanation is when my explanations could be played up big as some sort of coverup—or dismissed out of hand.

White: Responsible publishers such as *Readers Digest*, *National Geographic*, and the *New Yorker* make a habit of following up on the accuracy of their authors by asking us to check their factual material. But as far as the UFO books or the tabloid press—no, they've never checked with us before publishing....

Redmond: ... or after publishing, either!

Question: For the record, do you have any secrets about UFOs or alien life?

White: Not a bit. Those stories are garbage and I tell anybody who calls just that. Normally we don't want to dignify such trash with a serious response.

Redmond: We don't have any UFO secrets. As a matter of fact, this is an area where our office has spent more time digging out photographs and transcripts for the news media, in response to so-called "UFO claims." But as far as the suggestion that we're withholding anything, it's flat out not true.

White: We do know about cases where we have provided films and reports and technical studies and then seen that information twisted and give false impressions. That's where these stories about astronauts and UFOs come from: unverified or twisted information.

Question: Was there ever any capability to censor space transmissions?

Redmond: The Public Affairs Officer—the "P-A-O"—in Mission Control did have an inhibit switch for the air-to-ground voice signals, which were on a seven second delay to allow synchronization with the computer-processed television images...

White: ... but that switch was never used, to the best of my recollection. And I was a "voice of Apollo" PAO for many, many flights.

Redmond: Right, I suppose it was there to keep a space tragedy off the air "live" until we could notify any next of kin, but it would not in any case have affected the transcripts, only the real-time release which was piped to the newsroom and out to the networks. We only had authority to use it for a minute or so at most, anyway. The transcripts would eventually come out, completely uncensored.

White: Occasionally we would configure for private medical or family conversations. There was no special frequency or code, we'd just have the rest of the consoles get disconnected at the communications center.

Redmond: The medical conversations were not recorded, and were not released—although we would summarize them in press conferences. There's something in

61

the Hippocratic Oath about a doctor having to maintain confidentiality with his patients.

Question: How often did this happen?

Redmond: During Apollo, quite infrequently. During Skylab, we'd have such a talk maybe every three days or so.

Question: So there was no special code or secret channel?

Redmond: No, we used our ordinary channels, but the crew would request the doctor only—the "flight surgeon"—and the rest of us would disconnect.

White: Or else the crew could talk privately to their families in a back room down the hall from the control room.

Question: Outside of these confidential talks with doctors, wives, and children, were there any other conversations not publicly available?

Redmond: No, I don't think so, I don't see how they could have managed it.

Question: Why do you suppose those UFO books and magazine articles are written with such nasty accusations against NASA?

White: I think they're only written to exploit public hysteria, and to hell with the facts. That's my personal opinion, that they pander to panic, and appeal to public ignorance.

Redmond: I feel frustrated by the näivite of the public, and by the outright profiteering of writers who play on the public's desire to be mystified. But they just use cheap tricks, these writers. They deliver counterfeit goods.

Question: But what damage does it do?

White: Not much. Only a small fringe really believes such trash, considering the credibility of the sources.

Redmond: I disagree. I think it's quite harmful in reducing the credibility of the space program, and NASA's image.

Allow me a moment for a commentary of my own: A reader of this report will come to a conclusion altogether different from that espoused by Wilson, Harder, Barry, Gris, Berlitz, and others. A well-publicized collection of cranks, crackpots, con men and well meaning innocents have created a facade of 'UFO encounters' and a counterfeit claim of 'NASA coverup' concerning UFOs allegedly seen on the Apollo 11 moon expedition ten years ago. For some, the rewards are probably psychological, for others, publicity; for those portions of the news media which have eagerly offered them a forum, the juicy

GRENADA 35¢

UFO
RESEARCH INTO UNIDENTIFIED FLYING OBJECTS
VASARHELYI

1950

The Apollo 11 UFOs even were immortalized on postage stamps.

rewards have been financial in nature. Explanations and exposés (such as in the Fall and Winter 1977 *Search* magazine, the February, 1977 *Space World,* the 1978 issues of *the Skeptical Inquirer,* and official NASA news releases) are ignored or misrepresented—and here indeed is the real coverup conspiracy, if one can be said to exist. The reputation of the space program and of the astronauts has suffered, the public has been confused and misled, and the money rolls in. Where, I often wonder, are the courageous investigative journalists who will rip the lid off of this UFO scam?

Where does that leave readers after seeing what looked like a watertight space UFO story fall apart into mistakes, forgeries, and lies? Experienced UFO specialists must wonder how many other "classic" UFO cases which look equally as good are equally as rotten below the surface.

Two questions come to mind, but cannot be answered. First, wasn't Apollo 11 exciting *enough* without the fictionalized UFOs? And second, if there *are* so many other truly authentic UFO cases on record, why do the UFO writers have to rely so heavily on such shaky evidence as this?

The answers to these questions will help establish the true importance of what otherwise could only have been a squalid footnote to a historic chapter in space exploration. But whether future UFO researchers and enthusiasts will learn anything from it is a good question. For we can see that UFO stories seem to spring up and promulgate themselves, even when there is absolutely no foundation in fact on which they could have possibly been based. And if that is true in this case, we have to suspect that it has happened with some frequency in other cases where we can't determine the facts with such certainty. And much as they might like otherwise, the UFO experts and publicists—Mullaney, Sandler, Emenegger, Fuller, Hervey, Button, Harris, Binder, Matsumura, Barry, Pepper, Lorenzen, Harder, Chatelain, Lepoer-Trench, Zigel, Boznich, Wilson, Andrus, Gris, Goodavage, Beckley, Pratt, Creighton, Berlitz, Moore, Azhazha, and others have to somewhat be called to account for promulgating basically faulty standards. For no matter what they may admit in private, their public positions remain deceptive.

That is the true moral of the Phantom UFOs of Apollo 11!

Chapter Four
Myths and Mysteries of the Moon

The moon has many mysteries. Some are very old and some are new. Some are counterfeit. Some are very real. All are fascinating.

Every frontier seems to have developed its unique mythology. The wandering Greeks saw sirens and cyclopses and sought the Golden Fleece. Sailors thousands of years later reported sea serpents and mermaids. Strange civilizations were waiting beyond the known lands: Atlantis, the kingdom of Prester John, the Seven Cities of Cibola. Marvelous and miraculous artifacts were brought home and displayed. Unicorns and unipeds were just over the next hill.

These myths and legends often took centuries to develop and spread, as traveller's tales and minstrel's fables were combined, recombined, embellished and exaggerated. But today, an amazing new phenomenon has appeared: the legends and myths of the space frontier have sprung up almost overnight and are spreading around the world.

What are these myths about? Are they merely for entertainment, or are they in some way harmful? Why have they been ignored by the "establishment" science? Is there any truth to some of the weird and wild stories of outer space?

The moon, both before and after Apollo, has had a grip on the human imagination. It has provided its share of puzzles. Was it a mirror of the earth or an independent world with mountains and oceans of its own? What were the lights and glows seen from time to time upon its face? What was the hidden side like? Where did the surface features come from, and where did some of them vanish to?

Many eighteenth century astronomers were convinced that the moon was inhabited. Later in 1823, Gruithuisen announced he had seen a city which year by year was changing and expanding its outline. In the 1830s, the New York *Sun* ran a series of articles about the discovery of living creatures on the moon—later exposed as a clever and amusing hoax. More than a century later, some astronomers reported making out the shadow of a massive bridge spanning the rim of the Mare Crisium; other observers suggested it was an optical illusion caused by shadows on uneven ground. What was on the moon after all?

With the arrival of on-site lunar exploration in the 1960s, lunar scientists expected many answers. The more perceptive expected new mysteries as well. Nobody could have forecast the new hoaxes which followed in the wake of Apollo.

As the first data came back to earth from the Surveyors and Lunar Orbiters fifteen years ago, strange-looking structures were seen on the surface of the moon. They attracted the attention of the mass media and of UFO buffs in particular. As science fiction writers had long theorized, alien civilizations (even extinct terrestrial civilizations) may have left traces of their visits on the moon. As other observers theorized, life might even exist, either native or imported, on the moon right up until today.

One space photograph released by the National Aeronautics and Space Administration (NASA) showed what could only be described as a group of soaring spires, more than a hundred feet high, vaguely reminiscent of radio towers or even rockets standing on launch pads. What kinds of natural formations could have accounted for these objects? Could they be artifacts or even animals?

NASA scientists suggested that they were only large (twenty to forty feet across) boulders casting long shadows because of the low sun elevation, less than eleven degrees, about a day after lunar sunrise. The largest 'rock,' however, cast a disproportionately long shadow, indicating to many people that it was three or four times as high as it was broad. Such were the widely publicized reports, at least.

Later studies caused all serious observers to reconsider this estimate. Even authors such as Ivan Sanderson soon realized that the shadow was so long only because it was being cast downhill into a low-lying crater. When topographic corrections were

"Lunar animals and other objects, discovered by Sir John Herschel in his Observatory at the Cape of Good Hope and copied from sketches in the *Edinburg Journal of Science"* Lithograph by Benjamin H. Day, New York, 1835, based upon the Moon hoax perpetrated by the American journalist John Adam Locke in *The New York Sun*, 1835; in which the British astronomer Sir John Herschel (1792-1871) supposedly viewed life on the moon through his telescope. From the Library of Congress Division of Prints and Photos. Permission granted by Smithsonian Institution, Washington, D.C.

made, the shape of the object became unspectacular; it was thirty to forty feet wide and twenty to thirty feet high, easily within the normal shape of a big rock. There were no 'mysterious moon spires' after all!

But this explanation, like so many other solutions to 'strange and unknown' phenomena which 'baffle science' and which have 'no earthly explanation' was not widely reported. More accurately, I have never seen it printed anywhere, even though all the major analysts have privately come to that conclusion long ago. But instead of correcting earlier mistakes, the writers moved on to new areas of investigation.

In order to exploit the high public interest in moon expeditions and astronaut accomplishments, many sensationalistic writers combed the space reports looking for anomalous or strange occurrences or for any ordinary occurrences which could be made to look strange after appropriate alterations. As could be expected, many of them found exactly what they were looking for.

Most of the credit for setting off the modern moon hoaxes of the 1970s must go to author Joseph Goodavage, a prolific writer well known to UFO, parapsychological, and astrological audiences. He approached editor Martin Singer of *Saga* magazine with a story of alien civilizations on the moon, seen by our astronauts.

Goodavage's report was published in *Saga UFO Report* in 1974-75 in two sections: "What Strange and Frightening Discoveries Did Our Astronauts Make on the Moon?" and "Did Our Astronauts Find Evidence of Aliens on the Moon?" Excerpts from astronaut voice transcripts, interviews with scientists, and speculation by philosophers all seemed to provide overwhelming evidence of something strange going on around the moon.

In fact, the answers to Goodavage's two title-questions are "None at all" and "Not a bit," respectively, Goodavage seems to have deliberately re-edited the transcripts, raised questions he would have been an idiot not to have known the real answers to, and twisted the honest comments of naive scientists into something apparently sinister, ominous, and exciting.

Now these are serious accusations against a well known and widely read author. How can the average reader verify or refute the charges that Goodavage deliberately constructed a counterfeit mystery for motives as yet unknown?

Anyone familiar with space jargon is immediately struck by the fuss Goodavage makes over ordinary terms, and by Goodavage's published misconceptions and factual atrocities. "CAPCOM," says the author, means 'captain of communications,' and it refers to the astronaut in Mission Control who speaks to the crew in flight (actually, it stands for 'capsule communicator,' which any NASA offical could have told him). "EMUs and PLSSs," which Goodavage suggests are code words for alien artifacts, and simply abbreviations for "Extravehicular Mobility

Humankind's first steps on another world helped unleash a new wave of intellectual and scientific progress—and a new type of folklore, the whispered rumors of "outer space mysteries." Photograph courtesy of NASA

Units" and "Portable Life Support Systems," used on moonwalks. "Graben" is a common geologic term, not a UFO classification.

Goodavage also seems to have a bad memory and worse research habits. For instance, he describes Alan Shepard's 1961 space flight,"... precariously perched atop a Redstone rocket in an incredibly cramped Gemini capsule...It would be two long agonizing years before the first American would achieve earth orbit." It was, of course, a *Mercury* capsule, and it was only nine months before John Glenn made his ride into orbit.

But Goodavage's moon hoax was based on more than sloppy homework: the major evidence for aliens on the moon' is manufactured part and parcel from distorted Apollo voice transcripts by means of out-of-context selections, juxtapositions of unrelated comments, and (when it suits the purposes) what seems to be purely fictional phrases.

"Here's an example of what a rich harvest (the transcripts) yielded after many days of digging," boasts Goodavage, presenting this report from Apollo 16:

CAPCOM: You talked about something mysterious....
ORION: OK, Gordy, when we pitched around, I'd like to tell you about something we saw around the LM. When we were coming about thirty or forty feet out, there were a lot of objects, white things, flying by. It looked like they were coming—it looked like they were being propelled or ejected, but I'm not convinced of that....

"By what?" Goodavage demands. "By intelligent life from other worlds?"

Picture the scene Goodavage has conjured up: Two astronauts on the lunar surface, turning around to look at their lunar module and being startled to see a flight of white objects, UFOs, buzzing their landing site, propelled by rockets or something like that.

But Goodavage spent days reading the transcripts, so we can be sure he knows *exactly* what the answer to his questions are. He would have been a moron not to have realized the real meaning of the astronaut's comments, since it was right in the portion of the transcript he chose to *omit:*

On the Apollo spaceship, only four hours outbound from earth, and nowhere near the surface of the moon, the crew is reporting on the extraction of the lunar module from its booster rocket garage.

ORION: Okay, Gordy, when we pitched around I'd like to tell you a little bit about something we saw on the LM. When we were coming around about thirty or forty feet out

The Apollo-12 flight reportedly had numerous encounters with unidentified flying objects during their moon expedition in 1969. Were these authentic or just rumors? Photograph courtesy of NASA

we had a lot of white particles, looked like it was coming out from around the lunar module. Quite a number of them and as we got closer it looked to me that the primary—most of the particles were coming between the ascent propulsion tank over quadrant-1 and this omni-antenna. It looks like this was being jetted out from either some outgassing or something, and we assumed it's Mylar insulation, but not convinced of that.

The Apollo crew continued to describe the particles which where flaking off a panel on the side of the lunar module, and

Astronauts explore the Moon's surface: many people today do not believe the "official" accounts of the Apollo expeditions. Artwork by Teledyne Ryan, courtesy of NASA

which might have been an indication that fuel was leaking from one of the tanks. The discussion went on for half an hour, sporadically, and I don't see how Goodavage could possibly have missed or misunderstood it. The image which he conveyed to his readers, who trusted him, is an outright, purposeful, incontrovertible deceit.

Goodavage professes bewilderment and suspicion over the fact that the astronauts used 'code words' like Bravo, Hotel, Kilo, Romeo, and Whiskey to conceal what they were doing, when any radio operator could have told him that they were code terms for letters of the alphabet, letters used to designate map coordinates, crater sub-groups, film magazines for the cameras, and sample bags for moon rock and dust. Nobody who spent days, or even half an hour, reading the transcripts could possibly have any doubt of this.

What is the point in belaboring what should now be obvious. Goodavage used tricks and chicanery to conjur up a non-existent mystery for which he proposes nonsensical and unnecessary solutions. There are two reasons to drive this point in once again: first, Goodavage is a noted UFO mythologizer, and UFO buffs should be given an accurate idea about how far they can trust him; second, he set off a series of new moon hoaxes which are still gathering momentum, and every one of them turns back to his articles as their basis for facts.

Beyond the myth-making of the sensationalists, astronomers have been fascinated with the question of whether the face of the moon is changing. Over the past century they have sought evidence for contemporary physical alterations of lunar topographic features. After one famous false alarm, they may have found that evidence.

The crater Linné is a lonely dot on the plains of the Mare Serenitatis. In the late 1860s it became famous when an astronomer, comparing what he could see with charts made thirty years before, announced that the crater had vanished. In its place was only a shallow white depression.

As dozens of astronomers turned their telescopes on Linné, many theories were voiced. Some thought it had been a volcano which melted or exploded. Others suggested that the walls had collapsed in a moonquake. One desperate theorist even proposed that Linné had been hit by another meteorite.

The reported disappearance of Linné is a famous case of a moon mystery widely publicized in Fortean literature and in modern moon myths. Unfortunately, interested readers are now being denied the true solution.

Linné is still there. Photographs from Apollo 15 reveal that it is a very fresh (relatively speaking! It could be millions of years old.) impact creater about 1½ miles across, with steep sides, and surrounded by a bright ejecta field about five miles in diameter. There is no indication in the photographs that there has been any physical change at all since the time when the crater was formed.

How could the crater appear to vanish? The answer lies in its freshness and in the small instruments used by so many of the moon watchers in the nineteenth century, instruments for which a 1½ mile crater was barely at or beyond the limits of resolution.

Depending on sun angle, Linné can appear as a white patch with or without a mark in the middle, a wide shallow crater, a domed crater, a smooth white dome, and other aspects. As with the Martian canals being observed in the late 1800s, much of what was seen (or not seen) was in the mind of the beholder.

The man who made the first maps in the 1830s looked at Linné again after its reported disappearance, and wrote that he could see no change in its appearance. This tipped astronomers off, and they paid more careful attention to the illumination conditions. Within a few years, Linné 'looked' normal again, so normal that one disappointed observer proposed that it had 'changed back.'

The Apollo 15 photos show a quite ordinary impact crater, perhaps the freshest of its size ever photographed. Post-impact modification is slight and there is absolutely no sign of volcanism.

The surrounding white patch, misinterpreted by early observers as the floor of a much larger crater, led to the estimates of crater size of about four to seven miles across. *That* crater Linné never existed. The smaller, but very real, crater Linné stands as a stark monument "to the perils of misinterpreting visual lunar observations near the resolution limit of small Earth-based telescopes," according to geologist Richard J. Pike. It is just the kind of prosaic, disappointing solution too often deliberately hidden by the moon mythmakers.

Another very fresh moon crater, however, may actually have been seen at its birth. Space scientist Dr. Jack Hartung recently suggested that a medieval chronicle of a celestial event on July 28, 1178 A.D., may refer to the actual meteorite impact which created the twelve mile wide crater Giordano Bruno.

According to a report of Gervase of Canterbury, who interviewed the eyewitnesses, a group of five men were sitting out one evening watching the crescent moon shortly after sunset. Suddenly "the upper horn split in two" and from it "a flaming torch sprang up, spewing out, over a considerable distance, fire, hot coals, and sparks." The chronicle goes on to describe other visual effects associated with the event.

Hartung was fascinated with the report, and decided to search Apollo photographs for any fresh craters in the region of the reported 'flaming torch.' He also confirmed that the moon was indeed a crescent and was really visible just as the chronicle described it on the specified day.

One candidate immediately was found: the farside crater Giordano Bruno (36 N, 105 E—just over the eastern edge of the moon). It had a spectacular ray pattern indicating freshness, a pattern so spectacular that photoanalysts in the 1960s had overestimated its diameter by a factor of three. As a matter of fact, it has the largest ray-to-crater-diameter ratio of any crater on the moon, indirect and independent proof that it is the youngest crater on the moon.

If Bruno really is only eight hundred years old (and astronomers are still considering alternate explanations, as well as the chilling odds that the chance of it occurring when it did was only one in a million), the floor should be warmer than normal. Thermal measurements from unmanned orbiting probes could

Long shadows on the moon, seen by a robot scout ship in 1966, immediately led to speculation and controversy. Courtesy of NASA

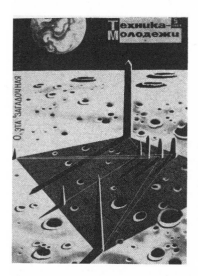

The Russians were convinced the objects were very tall. (This is the May 1968 issue of *"Technology-youth" magazine.*)

A fanciful view of the moon spires, based on American research. Courtesy of *Argosy* magazine

measure this. If it turns out to be that young, unmanned automatic moon rovers may some day be sent there to examine the actual location.

Linne and Giordano Bruno are the two most impressive examples of the search for newly changed lunar features. It is a real scientific effort, often hampered by unreliable observations and scanty data. It does not need sensationalistic mythmakers to hamper it further, or to try to make it any more exciting. The authentic mysteries are exciting enough.

On Earth, mountains take tens of millions of years to rise and fall. But the moon has just undergone a much more violent geological upheaval: An entire mountain range has vanished, only twenty years after it was first discovered.

It all began in October 1959 when the Russian space probe *Luna 3* looped around the hidden side of the moon and relayed photographs back to Earth. The images were blurry and washed out, but they did show some hitherto-unknown features, such as the Moscow Sea and the giant crater Tsiolkovsky. Although some skeptics proclaimed that the Russian photos were a hoax, subsequent U. S. probes confirmed their essential accuracy.

Well, not completely. On the *Luna 3* photos, a prominent linear feature was proudly labeled the Soviet Mountains (Montes Sovietici). But later U. S. probes, with better cameras, revealed that the area was in fact quite flat and that what had been interpreted as a towering mountain range was only a smear on the original blotchy photo.

But the Russians refused to concede their error, and as late as November 1978 they were still issuing lunar maps and charts with the Soviet Mountains firmly rooted in bedrock.

The issue came to a head at the seventeenth general assembly of the International Astronomical Union in Montreal in August 1979, with American space scientists digging in their heels against the Soviet scientists' insistence on official international blessing for the phantom mountain range.

When the Russians showed up, their maps no longer carried the name of the Soviet Mountains. Someone in Moscow seems to have decided it was a lost cause in the face of unsympathetic American scientists with suitcases full of Apollo photos of a flat, cratered plain where the mountain range should have been. But the Russians were not to go home empty-handed. They presented a list of eight new craters for the lunar far side, including one named Lipsky.

"Their maps show a nice, round, rimmed depression there," one American moon mapper remarked. "So we checked our

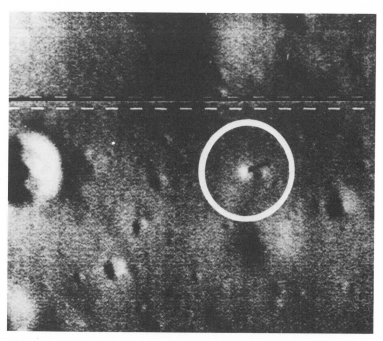

This pyramidal structure was spotted in the late 1960's. Courtesy of NASA

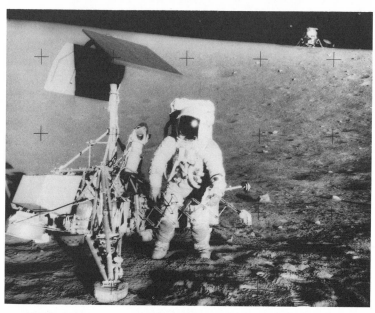

. . . it was a surveyor moon robot, much like this one visited by Apollo-12 astronauts in 1969. Courtesy of NASA

photos again. Nothing—there's no crater there at all! Maybe we'll call it the Lipsky Plains or something." Whatever the fate of the crater named Lipsky, the massive Soviet Mountains have evaporated into the mist of politics from which they originated.

The Japanese space program is continuing to gain momentum, and some experts are predicting that Japan will launch scientific moon probes within a few years. But according to the *National Enquirer,* a Japanese spaceman has already been out to the moon—in spirit, if not in body.

"Psychic Revealed Moon's Dark Side Before Anyone Ever Saw It," shouted the headline in the September 19, 1978, issue of the weekly tabloid. According to author John Cooke (like most NE staffers, an expatriate Britisher getting training in American tabloid press techniques), a Japanese psychic named Koichi Mita "mentally projected an image of the moon's dark side onto a photographic plate—twenty-six years before anyone ever saw it." The picture, which was made in November 1933 in Gifu City, Japan, was confirmed by the Russian moon probe Lunik-3 in October 1959, claims the article.

"Psychic" photographs are no strangers to skeptics, as witness the claims (and exposures) of Ted Serios, Uri Geller, Masuaki Kiyota, and others. What is novel about this new claim is that the photo was allegedly made decades before anyone knew what should have been seen there.

(To be picky, anyone can project an image on the moon's dark side onto any piece of film, since the moon's dark side is black, as is the color of exposed film. Cooke was simply confusing the popular, but incorrect, term "dark side of the moon" for the more correct "far side of the moon." Scientists sending photographic probes make sure that they pass over the target when the near side is dark and the far side is consequently sunlit; otherwise the photographs would not turn out.)

According to Japanese psychic researchers, the "thought" photograph (or "nengraph") had been held under strick controls since it was made. Unfortunately, no records of the original session seem to exist, since Gifu City was burned to the ground during an allied air raid in 1945, but somehow the photo survived. Why it should have been so carefully guarded is puzzling, since it is hard to imagine that its custodians would think that it would ever be verified. Flights to the moon were considered to be a century or more away.

The most disturbing aspect of the whole business is that the nengraph does look very much like one of the Lunik-3 photos, but there is one problem: the Lunik-3 photos do not look much like the

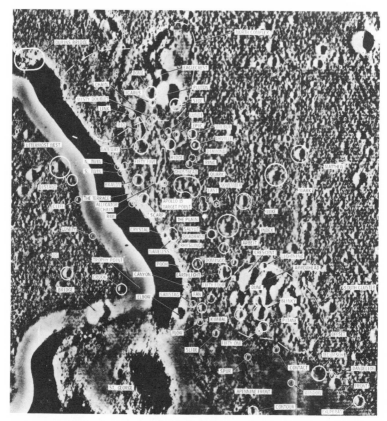

Complex astronaut jargon and weird place names often understandably confused the public. This is an Apollo-15 map of the Hadley Rille area. Courtesy of NASA

moon. As confirmed by later American flights, the Lunik-3 photos are of such poor quality, are so blotchy and washed out, and have so many extraneous features and errors (an entire mountain range, proudly called the "Soviet Mountains," turned out to be a data-transmission error), that they are poor reproductions of the actual view of the far side of the moon.

But there they are, blotches and all, on the alleged 1933 thought photograph. Not even considering the remarkable similarity of the two photos (the angle of view, range, lighting conditions, and numerous other variables are identical), the contents alone lead a skeptic to suspect that the purported 1933 nengraph is a clumsy forgery of the 1959 Russian photo, subsequently placed under the "strict controls" of the original (if, indeed, it ever existed). Such a trick is a classic one in the world of conjuring, particularly when enthusiastic scientists are the ones enforcing the controls.

"There's no room for any doubt in this case," asserted Toshiya Nakaoka, chairman of the Japanese Association for Psychotronic Research and allegedly director of the Fukurai Institute of Psychology in Niizakadori. (My letters sent to that address were returned "addressee unknown.") A psychic researcher for more than thirty years, Nakaoka was quoted as saying, "Mita gave a demonstration of two types of paranormal ability, out-of-body travel and nengraphy. There is no doubt this nengraph is the same one made in 1933."

But even proving that the 1933 nengraph (whenever it was really made) is actually a copy of the 1959 photograph and not really another view of the far side of the moon (since the actual date of the nengraph session was lost when the records were destroyed, it's impossible to compare the phases of the moon on the photos) will probably not dampen the enthusiasms of the psychic researchers. In that case, if Mita did not make an out-of-body voyage, he performed an even more astounding feat: precognition of the newspapers of 1959 that carried the Russian photo. QED, the paranormal world triumphs again.

But the myths and hoaxes continue. The topical and spiritual successor to Goodavage's moon hoax of 1975 is Don Wilson and his paperback books *Our Mysterious Spaceship Moon,* and *Secrets of Our Spaceship Moon* also widely excerpted in the UFO pulp magazines and newspapers. Wilson's techniques seem very similar to Goodavage's, and like all good students he has improved on his teacher. Take for example this Mercury-9 UFO sighting as 'reported' by Wilson:

> Cooper described the object as being of 'good size,' and claimed: "It was higher than I was. It wasn't even in the vicinity of the horizon...." This indicated that the bogey (NASA's slang term for UFOs) was not a star or other object, either natural or manmade.

Wilson has the chutzpah to actually give a true footnote on the source of Cooper's quotation, lending authenticity to the passage. Obviously he never expected anyone to check up on his footnote, because this is what they would have found:

At five hours into the Mercury flight, Cooper is reporting on *auroral* activity ('northern lights') in space: "Right now I can make out a lot of luminous activity in an easterly direction. I wouldn't say it was much like a layer. It wasn't distinct and it didn't last long, but it was higher than I was. It wasn't even in the vicinity of the horizon and was not well defined. A good size.... It was a good sized area. It was very indistinct in shape. It was a faint

INTERNAL STRUCTURE OF THE MOON

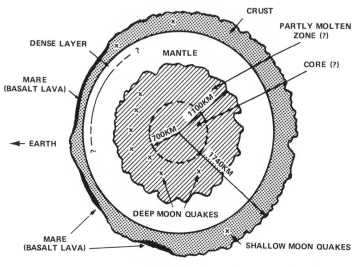

The interior of the moon, as revealed by Apollo data—not hollow! Credit: NASA

glow with a reddish-brown cast."

Cooper's words can in no way be construed to describe a conventional UFO—until Wilson is done distorting them. This is fraud, pure and simple. It is the reader who is being defrauded.

Cooper, who does believe that some UFOs are authentic and probably represent alien spacecraft, has all the same denounced the UFO accounts associated with his space missions. The fabled Mercury-9 UFO ("also seen by ground personnel," according to the late Frank Edwards) never existed, Cooper has asserted, and "I have the original on-board tapes in my possession" to prove it. The former astronaut went on (in a letter to me in early 1978): "I am really getting antagonistic at various people 'creating' whatever UFO stories they can link with whomever they want in order to make a profit."

The following year, in an interview with *OMNI* magazine, Cooper elaborated: "I've always been honest about my views on the subject. Because the astronauts have been so badly misquoted by irresponsible journalists, it's up to each of us to say what he believes in....It got so bad that there were deliberately falsified tapes of communications with the astronauts, where UFO material was simply edited in."

Wilson's main thesis is that the moon is a giant space ark, a

The crater Aristarchus has been the site of many mysterious "lunar transient phenomena" lights and hazes. Credit: NASA

hollow alien spacecraft. Two obscure Russians suggested this in a magazine article in 1970, and it must have looked like a good story. Unfortunately it is just not true—Wilson is totally unable to name any scientist who believes it, despite numerous allusions to 'many scientists' or 'numerous space specialists.' If Wilson had not presented so much distorted evidence in his book, he would probably be the only person in the West who believes the theory.

He writes as if he trusts all of Joseph Goodavage's moon hoaxes, so we can conclude that he never did any of his own original research. He asserts that it's "a mystery" why "craters are rare on earth . . . (while) the moon is a pockmarked world . . . Less than a score of such craters can be found on earth; millions on the moon." Wilson is just ignorant. The last decade has witnessed the discovery and investigation of the earth's equivalent of lunar craters—as documented in a dozen scientific and popular journals.

The crater Giordano Bruno, whose birth may have been witnessed in the Twelfth century A.D. Credit: NASA

Wilson tries to side step any possible criticism of his phony evidence with the UFO standard technique called "the Galileo Effect" gambit: "So-called modern scientific knowledge—concepts that have been entrenched for ages like old superstitions—are not uprooted easily. New ideas...are generally rejected offhand, and often with derision, and hostility...So too it will probably be with this concept."...You know it, Don!

In actual substance, just what is Wilson's much touted evidence that the moon might be hollow? When a reader examines the evidence carefully, piece by piece, it consists of pitifully weak and irrelevant 'facts' and fictions.

First, Wilson asserts that the moon is too "light" in weight unless it were hollow. Actually, as astronauts helped prove, the rocks from the moon show less density than those of earth because of some differentiation which was a feature of the births of the two neighboring worlds. The density through the moon can be accounted for by solid materials.

Next, Wilson quotes an American space expert who says the moment of inertia of the moon seems to indicate a core less dense than the crust. But the data was from 1962, before any American spacecraft had even reached the moon!

"Another study conducted by Dr. Sean C. Solomon of MIT claimed that latest data of the gravitational fields (sic) of the moon indicated that the lunar sphere could be hollow.... Solomon concluded that the Lunar Orbiter findings indicated 'the frightening possibility that the moon might be hollow.'"

I looked up the vaguely referenced article in 'The Moon,' Jan.-Feb. 1974, pp. 147-65, and found these concluding words: "The lunar orbiter experiments vastly improved our knowledge of the moon's gravitational field, especially considering that the classical value for (the moment of inertia) indicated the frightening possibility that the Moon might be hollow...."

Now what does this mean? It implies just the opposite of what Wilson claims it does.

Much of the supporting evidence for the "hollow moon" theory allegedly came from the book *Our Moon* by H. Percy Wilkins, a British moon expert (not to be confused with a British UFO enthusiast of the 1950s named "H. Wilkins"). The book was extremely difficult to obtain (try it yourself: it was published in London in 1958 by Frederick Muller, Ltd), but an interlibrary loan request finally found a dusty copy at the University of Oregon in Eugene. It had been read numerous times when it had first come out, but since 1963—when the real moon data began coming in from space probes—it had not been checked out a single time until my request. Yet Wilson considers it one of his best, most up-to-date sources of supportive information!

Nonetheless, the search was worth it. It showed again how blithely Wilson seems to have rearranged—even reversed—the scholarly footnotes he presented to his readers.

Case in point: Wilson claimed that Wilkins said, "Every indication is that the moon, thirty miles beneath its crust, is hollow." What Wilkins really wrote was that "everything points to the more or less hollow nature of the crust of the moon, within

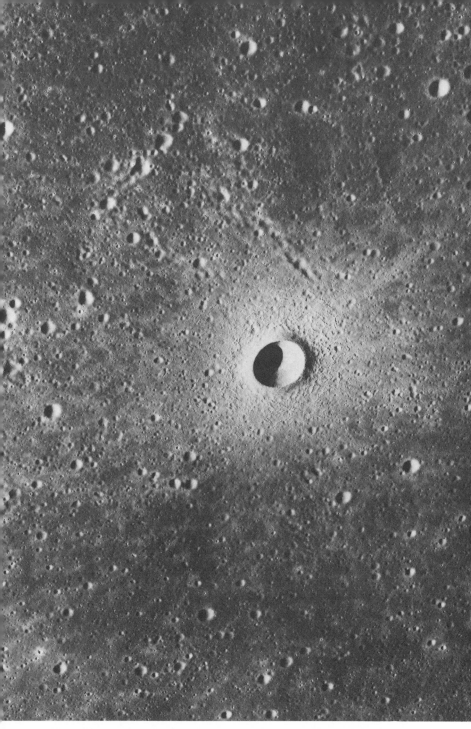

Linné Crater, which appeared to disappear in the nineteenth century. But it's still there, with no sign of dynamic activity. Credit Lunar and Planetary Institute

some twenty or thirty miles of the surface (p. 120): (Wilson occasionally quotes it correctly but out of context, too.) Wilson claimed that Wilkins said that these hollows (which Wilkins thought to be natural caverns) could amount to "no less than fourteen millions of cubic miles" (that is about 2% of the moon's volume). What Wilkins actually wrote (pp. 119-20) was: "Long ago it was calculated that if the moon had contracted on cooling at the same rate as granite, a drop of only $180°F$ would create hollows in the interior amounting to no less than fourteen millions of cubic miles....However, it is unlikely that the moon contracted at the same rate as granite; it is almost certain that nothing like fourteen millions of cubic miles of cavities were formed...." Wilkins concluded (p. 123) that "the moon, then, would seem to be a world, doubtless cold and solid in the centre, but honey-combed near the surface beneath the giant craters and domes." This was a reasonable supposition for the 1940s and the 1950s, and is now known to be not true—but an authentic report of Wilkins' theories in no way could support Don Wilson's wild ideas, so Wilson took extensive liberties with Wilkins' ideas.

In a way, the hollow moon books are masterful examples of scholastic fraud, and show great skill, imagination, and effort on the part of their author. It's too bad he chose such an obviously crackpot idea—if he had used the same techniques in politics, economics, or religion, he might have written a classic which could have been seriously debated in academic circles for decades!

Wilson's first book did not make much of a splash outside the world of UFO enthusiasts (serious ufologists thought it was nonsense, too—but somehow their followers never got the unambiguous word to that effect). A favorable review did appear in the Lewiston (Maine) *Daily Sun* in mid-1979: "Don Wilson has come up with some very interesting facts that support life in outer space." But the only other paper that seems to have reviewed it is the West Chester (Pennsylvania) *Local News,* whose editor complained that "the book is sloppily written and poorly edited. It is so repetitious it might make the reader wonder whether the author slapped together notes and fragmentary writings." There were few other ripples in the real-world but the book's greatest influence has already been felt on subsequent UFO books and magazine articles, which have been using it as a reliable data source.

And now comes the best part, so get ready for a laugh. Just who are Vasin and Shcherbakov, the great Soviet scientists from the Academy of Science who are the originators of the 'hollow

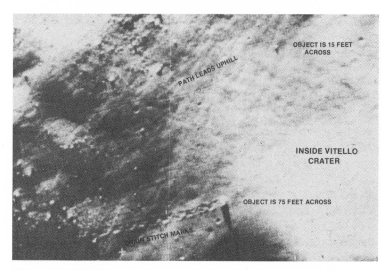

Labels in image: PATH LEADS UPHILL · OBJECT IS 15 FEET ACROSS · INSIDE VITELLO CRATER · OBJECT IS 75 FEET ACROSS · STITCH MARKS

Three tabloid headlines show how popular Leonard's theories became.

moon?'

Any attempt to find these names in standard reference works such as "Who's Who in Soviet Science," "Who's Who in Russia," or data bases of all scientific papers published in the USSR in the past twenty-five years is bound to fail, as I found out when I made those searches. I can find no Soviet scientists of any renown who go by those names.

Their true status was revealed early in 1977 when I received an amazing piece of information from colleagues at the prestigious Vernadskiy Institute in Moscow. I was told that Vasin was a journalist specializing in engineering and space topics. Shcherbakov was a friend of his. They have never been associated in any way with the prestigious Academy of Sciences.

But the most astounding part of the letter disclosed that the "hollow moon theory" was entirely a joke! It was a spoof! The article was written for a scientific journal as humorous relief, as a tongue-in-cheek satire on the later discredited suggestion of Josef Shklovskiy that the moons of *Mars* are hollow space vehicles of enormous size.

What Vasin and Shcherbakov set out to do in their humorous put-on was to show just how wild a space theory could get and still *not* be disprovable in any rigorous sense. The theory was never a serious one and the scientists, who read it in manuscript form, realized it so the authors could stack the deck in order to show how easily it could be done.

87

They succeeded beyond their dreams, since a Moscow editor of 'Sputnik' (the Soviet equivalent of *Reader's Digest*) thought it was an authentic example of Soviet scientific breakthroughs, a thought provoking and exciting idea. The hoax got out of hand when it was translated into the English-language edition. By the time author Don Wilson fell for the satire, and wrote his books it was no longer funny and a lot of readers have been misled.

Retired government health worker George Leonard, living in the Maryland suburbs of Washington, D.C., has claimed that somebody else is on the moon: Not artifacts, not traces of past activity—but present occupation of the moon by an intelligent alien civilization, right in front of our eyes. UFOs on earth are ships from the moon, Leonard believes.

An amateur astronomer, Leonard had long been fascinated by mysterious lights seen on the moon. While most astronomers consider them obscure natural events (and we'll discuss them later), Leonard is convinced that the only explanation is that they are traces of the activities of his secret moon inhabitants.

When the first moon photos were sent back by American space probes, Leonard carefully searched them for signs of alien artifacts which he already expected were there. He spent weeks staring at the photographs on file at the Public Information Office at NASA headquarters in Washington. Amid the lights and shadows of the harsh lunar landscape (not 'terrain,' to be accurate, but 'lurain!'), Leonard found what he was looking for.

He "located" manufactured objects, towers, platforms, cranes, hieroglyphics, trap doors, pipes, and other objects, some of them miles in size. Once he found them, he realized that NASA, too, must have seen them. Since the space agency has never announced such discoveries, and since space officials profess ignorance, bewilderment, amusement and annoyance when he tries to make them admit it, the only logical conclusion is that NASA is deliberately covering up some evidence.

In fact, just like the astronomers who mapped hundreds of Martian canals—imaginary, non-existent canals—two generations ago, Leonard has been seeing things which aren't there, created by illusions of debris, crevices, shadows, ejecta blankets, wall slumping, and miscellaneous detritus. The simple truth is that there is nobody else on the moon. Not one of Leonard's hundreds of catalogued objects exists.

The quality of reprinted photographs is insufficient for any reader to verify that the artifacts are or are not there. Anyone who wants to check up Leonard and me must obtain his or her own prints.

Two boulders left tracks on the surface, as seen by unmanned "lunar orbiter" in the late 1960s. Credit: NASA

Boulder tracks down a mountainside seen out the window of Apollo-17 on the surface, December 1972.

Leonard's problem was that he knew practically nothing about how moon scientists were analyzing and distributing the lunar data. He had read a few clippings, haunted the headquarters Public Information Office, visited the nearby Goddard Space Center, and claims to have flown to California to interview a renegade ex-NASA scientist who confessed the whole coverup ("Dr. Sam Wittcomb" is the pseudonym of an apparently entirely fictitious character which Leonard should have saved for a science fiction novel, not a book alleged to be based on fact). But Leonard had never heard of the top American moon study center, the Lunar and Planetary Institute adjacent to NASA's Johnson Space Center in Houston. Worse, he was satisfied to use publicity photographs which were several generations degraded from the original crystal clear moon pictures—Leonard did not even seem to know there were crystal clear moon pictures.

I visited the Lunar & Planetary Institute (next door to the Johnson Space Center south of Houston) to track down the original prints of the shots Leonard claimed he could see artifacts in. The artifacts were not there. I telephoned Leonard to inform him of my discovery of higher quality photographs, and he asked me how his moon machines look in the better pictures. There was a mixture of disappointment and distrust in his voice when I told him that the moon machines evaporated in the cold light of reality. When I told him that I was working in the NASA space program myself, he immediately decided I was part of the NASA coverup and that he could safely disregard my advice as part of a secret campaign to discredit him.

In the photographs, which I encourage everyone to examine for themselves, there are no traces of artificial objects. A "super rig" a mile high was only a pile of boulders near a crater wall. A "latin cross" was a debris mount (Leonard omitted, out of ignorance rather than deception, additional photographs which showed overhead closeups of the region.) "Rolling boulders" were just that. A "ladder" was only an ordinary crater chain. A "pure energy entity" turned out to be precisely what Leonard said it could not be: a splotch of white dust on the rim of a crater. A "manufactured object" on the floor of a crater is only a landslide.

Amazed readers should not take my word for it, since they would only be exchanging one authority for another. Instead, go buy the high quality prints from the Space Sciences Data Center, or visit the archives in Houston or Washington or Flagstaff. Either Leonard or I need to have our eyes—and head—

examined, and a curious reader should judge for himself or

Leonard also refers to excessive seismic activity caused by his lunarian civilization(s). Such activity does not exist. The moonquakes heard by the ALSEP seismic sensors are very weak; they even detected the footsteps of the astronauts who had turned them on.

At the photo interpretation laboratory in the annex building at the LPI south of Houston, specialists had spent some time before the Apollo landings searching the orbital photographs for boulder tracks. They wanted to determine the nature of the surface, how strong it was, how easily it was packed down, how sticky it was. During moonquakes and impacts eons ago, rocks and had been jarred or thrown loose from mountainsides, bouncing and rolling downhill.

During this search, the analysts accidentally came across a photo of a tiny artificial pyramid only six feet high. It turned out, of course, to be one of the Surveyor robots landed on the moon in 1966. Leonard claims that careful searches like this must have missed his moon machines thousands of feet high, or else that all the moon scientists (none of whom he had ever met) are one and all a pack of liars.

Time and again Leonard shows how meagre is his grasp of ordinary scientific concepts, and how deep seated in his loathing of 'establishment scientists.' He says we do not pick up the lunarian radio traffic because they may use different voice frequencies than those audible to the human ear. He forgets—or never learned—that the radio frequencies of a signal carrier have nothing really to do with the frequencies of the sound pattern they are carrying, and that we could hear or detect the radio signals no matter what the configuration. But the moon is radio-wise dead, dead, and quiet. Again, many times he refers to dirt-moving devices which operate like vacuum cleaners or snow blowers, not for a moment pausing to realize why a vacuum cleaner would not function in the lunar vacuum.

Checking up on the book's claims, a skeptical reader is ultimately driven to the dilemma of two unpleasant verdicts: sloppiness or incompetence. Genuine puzzles seem deliberately distorted, such as the sighting on Apollo 17 of a light flash on the moon. Leonard claims it could not have been caused by cosmic rays hitting the pilot's retina, a common space effect"…not has the Light Flash Phenomenon from cosmic rays ever confused the highly trained astronauts," he asserts. In fact, if he had bothered to do original research and read the actual flight transcript, or listened to the actual voice tapes (as I have), he would discover that the astronauts were discussing the possibility that the Light Flash Phenomenon was indeed the cause of the flash they had seen, although nobody was sure.[45] They were indeed confused.

The David McKay Publishers were so confident in the commerical possibilities of Leonard's book that they took out a double column ad for it in the October 24, 1976 *New York Times Book Review* section. Hypes the blurb: "Evidence the government has suppressed reveals unmistakable signs of underground life, massive structures, and vast machines at work on the Moon." The evidence is "incontrovertible," says the ad: "What the astronauts reported and what the photographs actually show have been discussed inside NASA, but officials will not talk about it publicly. The astronauts themselves used code words in describing many things they saw, but the purpose and meaning of these code words has been kept secret...."Evidently *Publishers Weekly* liked the book, because they supplied a quotation used at the end of the advertisement: "Leonard makes a detailed presentation of the 'evidence' for the existence of extraterrestrials on the moon. He has spent years studying key photos—of Tycho, King Crater, the Bulliadus-Lubinicky area—....His photos, to which he has added his own drawings for clarity and emphasis, are truly mind-boggling when one begins to see what he sees: immense 'rigs' apparently 'mining' the moon; strange 'geometricities,' markings, symbols, lights, evidences of change and movements."

Examination of printed photographs is difficult because of the reduction in clarity required for book production. So beginning in 1976 I issued a series of "no-lose guarantees" challenges to Leonard and/or anyone else who believes "somebody else is on the moon." Pending an agreement between our two parties, anybody who wants to can go and buy their own copies of these disputed photographs—and if they see what Leonard claims is there, I'll reimburse them all expenses (but if they can't see what Leonard claims is there, *he* pays their expenses). Funning thing is—in five years, nobody has agreed to pick up the other side of this challenge!

(In mid-1981 Leonard wrote to me and asked me not to publicly criticize his book anymore, implying it had been an honest mistake. Although the book is out of print, it is still being circulated, quoted, and used as a reference—so in light of Leonard's unwillingness to publicly say the book was wrong, I feel compelled to publish a refutation of it.)

The greatest mystery of the moon remains the reports of lights and shadows on the surface, which come and go

Author confers with George Leonard in his suburban Washington, D.C. home.

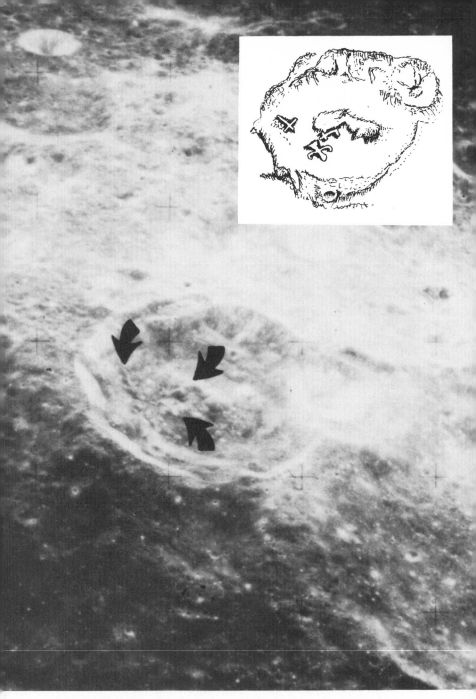

Resurrected "Moon machine" photos were being distributed in 1981 in California. George Leonard called this a "T-scoop cutting away central mountain . . . ," but recently recanted his whole book and wants to forget the entire thing.

Insert: This is what some people think they can see in this crater—

94

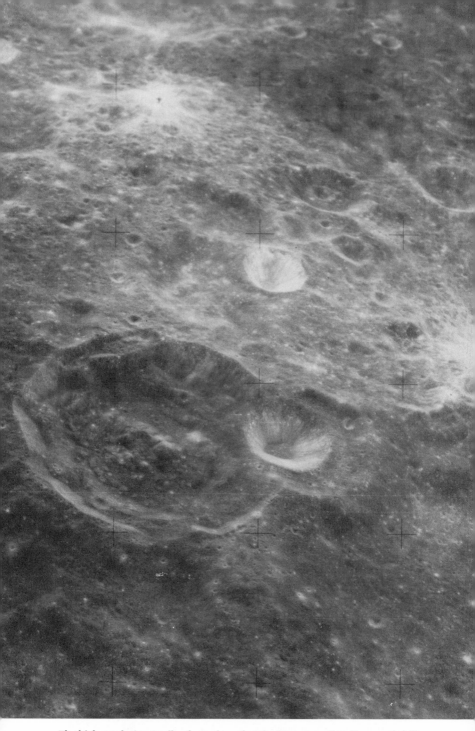

The high-resolution Apollo photo show that the "structures" really are only hills, crevices, and craters. Credit: Lunar and Planetary Institute

unexpectedly. Called 'Lunar Transient Phenomena' (LTP), they consist of hundreds of documented cases of glows, flashes, obscurations, mists, and colored patches. Scientists take them quite seriously and have a number of theories. They also know a lot more about them than the moon hoaxers like to admit.

The distribution of LTP sightings is not random, showing a preference for the edges of the lunar maria or a few young craters (there are very few reports from the lunar highlands), suggesting a volcanic connection. There are no coincidences between the most active LTP sites and any of the moonquake regions charted by the ALSEP stations, nor have the ALSEP ion detectors found any correlation with LTP either. The crater Aristarchus accounts for a third of all reports with other sightings in Alphonsus, Schroter's Valley, Piton Mountain, Plato, Dawes, and Posidonius.

Several possible causes of LTP have been suggested, and since the phenomenon manifests itself in so many different ways, several of the theories could be right simultaneously. Tidal effects might release internal gases such as those spectroscopically analyzed by Kozyrev in 1958; sunrise effects and other effects of low-angle illumination on surface glass could account for some brightenings; the earth's magnetosphere brushing against the moon, either as a magnetic tail, a magnetopause, or a bow shock, could excite lunar ions to luminescence in a manner similar to the aurora borealis ("northern lights") on earth. Direct solar plasma interactions with the lunar surface, caused by solar flares, is also suggested.

Apollo added much data to the question of dust activity near the moon. Although the moon does not have a real atmosphere, tiny particles are constantly being driven off the surface by solar radiation. Observations by astronauts in orbit showed sunbeams before orbital sunrise, indicating the presence of suspended dust clouds. An instrument called the Lunar Ejecta and Micrometeorite (LEAM) sensor was left on the moon as part of one ALSEP station and it confirms the presence of dust particles moving away from the sunlit side of the moon at dawn and dusk. Orbital detectors have spotted transient belches of gas from the lunar interior.

A special session of the Seventh Annual Lunar Science Conference in 1976, hosted by the Lunar Science Institute in Houston, was devoted to "Recent Activity on the Moon." Both moonquakes and LTP were discussed, and physical links between latent volcanism, extra-lunar triggering mechanisms, and visual observations were analyzed. An evening seminar which I personally attended was devoted to a lively discussion and debate about LTP.

In concluding that LTP must be an artificial phenomenon, not a natural one, the moon hoaxers are in the same frame of mind as the primitive savages who watched a thunderstorm, did not understand it, and concluded that the gods were making thunder and lightning. Natural explanations are sabotaged and any real attempt to solve the mysteries is derailed.

And no list of moon hoaxes would be complete without the claim that the entire Apollo program is a fake. This concept, being promoted by a West coast author, is having a little trouble getting accepted by the news media. (It seems that there *are* certain standards.) Santa Cruz, California, writer William Kaysing is trying to convince people that the entire Apollo moon program never happened.

There have always been people who could never believe that men have walked on the moon. The U.S. Information Agency took an opinion poll a few years ago in a number of Latin American, Asian, and African countries. They discovered that most people had not even heard of the moon flights, that many who had heard of them dismissed them as propaganda or science fiction, and that many of those who did believe that men had been to the moon were convinced that it had been the Russians! But even in North America and Europe, a fringe element has claimed all along that the moon flights were faked.

Kaysing believes (or professes to believe) that astronauts actually never step into the Saturn rockets at Cape Kennedy, but actually are whisked away to Nevada while the world watches the launch of an empty space capsule. Hollywood special effects men (and we know how good they are!) create the moon TV scenes somewhere in Arizona. When it is time to return, the men get into another capsule which is dropped from a high flying cargo plane so it can float into the view of the newsmen. The moon rocks are not from the moon at all: "You can pick them up anyplace—a meteorite, a piece of rock from the earth," Kaysing says, "They're common."

Kaysing may have moon rocks in his head, but the idea is fun to think about. It is trivially easy to refute point by point, but like all good hoaxes it will be impossible to stamp out, as it returns every few years to puzzle and mislead new generations of readers.

Moon mythologizers of the 1970s have claimed a spiritual ancestor in a character named Morris K. Jessup, a UFO writer of the 1950s. In *the Case for the UFO* (1955, Citadel, NYC) and *The Expanding Case for the UFO* (1957, Citadel, NYC), Jessup outlined a series of lunar mysteries which convinced him that the moon was a base for UFOs. Wilson and Leonard lean very heavily on Jessup's exhaustive list of lunar phenomena which seemed to indicate intelligent activity far out in space. Jessup, meanwhile, leaned heavily on the catalogs of Charles Fort, who had filled several books with data he claimed science had deliberately ignored (this, a generation before Jessup's books).

Wilson calls Jessup a "noted astrophysicist and mathematic- ian," a "renowned scientist" and similar praises. This is a buildup for an obscure astronomy student instructor from the midwest who has published only two short scientific papers in his whole career. Jessup was with the astronomy department of the University of Michigan in the 1920s, and dropped out of a doctoral program in 1931. He spent the rest of his life as an auto parts salesman in Washington, D.C.

Jessup was a mysterious character who appears now and then in the pseudo-science literature as a source of strange stories. Charles Berlitz (Without a Trace, 1977) connects him with the Carlos Allende fantasy of the 'Philadelphia Experiment' disappearing destroyer in World War II. Jessup's suicide at age 58 on May 20, 1959, when he was found dead in his station wagon with a hose from the exhaust in the window, has achieved the mythic status of a "termination with extreme prejudice' by either UFO invaders or government secret agents.

One basic question about these kinds of stories is: really, what harm do they do? Perhaps these theories are amusing and entertaining; perhaps few people really believe them anyway. So who is hurt by these harmless fables and fairy tales?

There is an old Kentucky proverb that answers this. It goes this way: "It ain't what you don't know what'll hurt you—it's what you do know what ain't so."

And that is the heart and essence of the problem. It is never funny to be misinformed. In our modern technological society, ignorance and delusions about science, and a lack of the ability to tell truth from falsehood, can lead people to wrong decisions which they, or their entire society, may have to pay dearly for.

If only a handful of people want to believe that the moon is hollow, who is hurt? If the Hare Krishna people believe that space flight is impossible, so does the Flat Earth Society (alive and well in 1981!), and they deserve each other.

But this avoids the question, since even those who do not really believe the myths have at least heard of many of them (or of others I haven't documented), and they may therefore lump the myths and the facts together as just two differences of legitimate

FALCON

An actual artificial object photographed on the moon's surface: the Apollo-15 lunar module, July 1971. Courtesy NASA

On the ridge of this crater, wrote George Leonard, are "x-drones making spiral cut" (in his chapter entitled "pushing the moon around: super rigs"). Credit: NASA

A recent California drawing of the X-drone machines (bottom) looks for all the world like a lost pile of Purina cat chow (top). Courtesy Mark Gaines and Jim Safran.

opinion. The truth, these people may suppose, "probably lies somewhere in between." And they miss the truth.

There is another factor, involving education. Many young people, especially those with a strong interest in science and space, do not have the perspective or the guidance to see through the hoaxes. Instead, they may take them very seriously indeed (and I speak from personal experience!) Some of them may be permanently imprinted with such pseudo-sciences and may waste years of intellectual effort. Others may throw the baby out with the bath water when they discover they've been duped. Most eventually will mature and will grow out of their naivité through reading and discussing things and developing their critical faculties. Some, however, can and will be intellectually scarred for life with the bitter disillusionment that comes with learning that somebody you trusted, or a book in which you had thought you had glimpsed the truth, was brazenly lying to you. That is not funny and it is not harmless.

The appeal of the moon myths seems to be that they are understandable while real science and real space exploration are not. In a sense, they are 'surrogate science,' useful to give the illusion of mental activity and intellectual pursuits. Most people are not very confident in their abilities to understand modern science, and the blame lies with education and with the news media.

This intellectual retreat from authentic science cannot be considered but as a detriment—and those forces which encourage and accelerate this abdication, may be guilty of absolute harm in a society such as ours where some basic scientific information *and* judgment can and must be mastered by the citizenry, both as voters and as consumers.

If the moon myths in themselves are not so damaging, the atmosphere which allows them to flourish and often triumph is certainly an intellectually crippling one, all too reminiscent of the bizarre irrational and anti-science cults which preceded the fall of democratic Germany in the 1930s. Such irrationality and non-rationality must not be tolerated, humored, or laughed at. The professional moon mythmakers should be put out of their lucrative business by vigorous confrontations with the truth, to make falsehood unprofitable.

The puzzle of the origin of the moon continues, but it is not true that "the great mysteries of the moon have come no closer to solution....One can search the scientific reports of the Apollo flights in vain and still not find a serious inroad to these mysteries...." (Leonard) The real nature of the moon, and the restrictions it puts on any theory of origin, are better understood every year. New pieces to the puzzle are found; old pieces are discovered to have been parts of another puzzle and are discarded. The facts are already exciting. The pity is that the people who are fed the fantasies would probably enjoy the facts better.

The moon has many mysteries. Some are very old and some are new. Some are counterfeit. All are fascinating, especially when the boycotted facts are added, and the fabulists and falsifiers are identified and confronted. The unique mythology of the moon today is artificial and phony; the unique and authentic scientific challenges of the moon today are exhilarating and intellectually satisfying.

Chapter Five
The UFO Hoax in Perspective

If UFO disbelievers are frequently too eager to dismiss UFO evidence as delusions and hoaxes, UFO believers for their part can tend to the other extreme: insisting on the utter trustworthiness of human testimony and on the alleged ease with which hoaxes can be exposed.

This question of hoaxes is an interesting aspect of the UFO phenomenon. It can serve as a test of the adequacy of UFO investigations, as a measure of the powerful "will to believe" on the part of many UFO investigators and authors, and as testimony to the imagination, humor, and daring of would-be hoaxers. Only when—and if—these lessons are fully appreciated will serious UFO investigators be able to escape insinuations and suspicions that they are frequently victimized, willingly or unwillingly, by hoaxes.

Some very revealing "UFO controlled experiment" hoaxes were engineered by English physicist David I. Simpson several years ago. According to his report published in the Spring 1980 issue of *Skeptical Inquirer,* the tests had "the aim of comparing known details of fabricated 'UFO' stimuli with the issued statements of investigators." In addition, Simpson wanted to test the abilities of UFO researchers by leaving clues which could be tracked to a solution: the hoaxes "were designed to present substantial inconsistencies that would allow any moderately critical investigator to cast strong suspicion on their authenticity."

One particular test hoax was executed on the evening of March 28, while a group of English UFO enthusiasts near Warminister were watching for UFOs which reportedly frequent that region. Simpson had a purple spotlight set up on a neighboring hill, and as it suddenly flashed on and off he had a bogus "magnetic detector" sound an alarm at the observation site. An accomplice with a camera containing pre-exposed film (which already showed UFO images!) made several exposures of the horizon and then handed the camera—the film still inside—to a leading UFO researcher in the group.

Simpson had prepared the hoax film so that the photographed direction and appearance of the "UFO" were grossly at odds with the actual visual stimuli. He had also seen to it that the first two pre-exposed frames (taken almost a year earlier) showed background scenes significantly different from the two subsequent real exposures (which of course did not show a UFO). This should have been apparent to an investigator.

But nobody seemed to notice (and nobody even interviewed the photographer). After two months of study by top UFO experts in Europe, the photographs were declared by *Flying Saucer Review* editor Charles Bowen "to be genuine beyond all doubt." One consultant reported that "there is nothing about these photographs which suggests to me that they have been faked in any way." UFOlogist Dr. Pierre Guerin, director of research at the Astrophysical Institute of the French National Center for Scientific Research, reported that "there is no question of the object photographed being in any possible way the result of faking."

An artist's impression of the UFO appeared on the cover of the July-August 1970 issue of *Flying Saucer Review*; it showed the "object" with an angular diameter ten times too large (the experts had computed that the flying saucer was sixty feet long and thirty feet in diameter). Eyewitness accounts described how the UFO—purple, fringed in white, with a crimson light in the middle—hovered momentarily and then moved towards the town before stopping again. Estimates of direction and duration were significantly in error, and the the errors accumulated as time passed (later, the object was described as giving off ultraviolet light and being surrounded by a "ruby-red halo").

Simpson's critique of the "investigation" (which he allowed to continue for 2½ years before revealing the hoax) was devastating: "My experiences in the UFO field have shown that the investigator incompetence demonstrated by this particular experiment, far from being exceptional, is typical... occasionally,

This hoax alien photo was published in an April Fools Day issue of a German newspaper in 1950 (Klaus Webner tracked it down in 1981).

individuals with relevant technical backgrounds become involved; it is disturbing to witness the abandonment of their mental disciplines and common sense....If ever there is subtle evidence suggesting extraterrestrial visitation, it is unlikely to be discovered by a typical UFOlogists."

Some UFO hoaxes start as impulsive pranks rather than carefully-planned scientific experiments. In March 1968, several college students at the University of Maryland were listening to a call-in radio show interview with a man who claimed to have been taken by saucer people to visit their home planet, Lanulos, "in the distant constellation of Ganymede." One of the students, Tom Monteleone, an avid science-fiction fan, picked up the phone to call and ask a question—but (as he later recalled) he suddenly thought, "Just for the heck of it, why not claim I've been to Lanulos too? It'll blow his mind!"

And so he did—and it did. The "contactee," Woodrow Derenberger, was initially dumbfounded but quickly regained his composure and agreed with all of Monteleone's descriptions of the planet Lanulos, even details which contradicted things Derenberger had just disclosed on the radio show. After fifteen minutes the college student hung up and enjoyed a good laugh with his roommates—until the phone rang. The radio station had traced his call and now wanted more details.

For the next two years Monteleone went along, proudly providing UFO investigators with information gleaned from Derenberger's accounts and from the general UFO literature. Whenever he thus "corroborated" earlier information, his credibility rose further. (He had told investigators that he was unfamiliar with UFO literature, so they believed him.) UFO publicist Harold Salkin was impressed that his story was "so tightly synchronized" with Derenberger's; UFO writer and editor Timothy Green Beckley taped an interview with Monteleone and wrote several magazine articles presenting the account as factual; noted UFO author and theoriest John Keel called the story "one of the most puzzling contact stories in my files...I'm forced to accept that it's true" (even though, as Monteleone noted, Keel's published accounts of the story were highly distorted).

"I underwent long interviews," Monteleone himself recounted in Omni (May 1979). "I not only repeated my false experiences but also added further embellishments and absurdities—just to see how far I could carry the hoax before being discredited." Monteleone even submitted to a hypnosis session sponsored by Salkin, during which he faked the trance and "passed" the test like a champ.

UFO antagonists Oberg and Timothy Beckley square off before an all-night radio talk show with "Long John" Nebel and Candy Jones, WMCA, New York, in January 1978.

Strangely enough, in late 1980, when the full admission of the hoax was published in *Fate* magazine (*Omni* had scooped them by a year and a half), Monteleone was the one blamed for all the confusion. His actions, wrote author Karl Pflock, "have served to muddy still further the already very muddy waters of UFOlogy. The last thing we need if we are to unravel the UFO mystery is false leads that absorb any part of the far-too-limited resources of serious researchers." (Among which he apparently considered Salkin, Beckley, Keel and others.) This ironic complaint appeared to absolve the over-gullible investigators of any responsibility for careless and credulous acceptance of Monteleone's deliberately-absurd fabrications.

Other reactions to Monteleone's confession are also amusing. Salkin, who is described by long-time UFOlogical observer James Moseley as "a warm, likable, but somewhat gullible sort," still refuses to believe Monteleone's confession. John Keel was particularly upset and issued a statement calling the *Fate* piece "an attempt to discredit my entire body of work and my professional reputation as a journalist for over thirty-five years" and is reportedly preparing a lawsuit. The accusation has been made in some circles that Monteleone's original Lanulos story is true but that he is falsely denying it for the sake of publicity.

As for Timothy Green Beckley, he has to worry about fresher wounds in his credibility as a competent UFO investigator. In a 1980 issue of his monthly tabloid newspaper, *UFO Review,* Beckley apparently became the victim of yet another UFO hoax.

In an article entitled "Erotic Encounters of the Very Close Kind," Beckley opened with the startling words: "It is not uncommon for the occupants of UFOs to have sexual contact with humans." He tried to lay the foundation for this far-out story in an editorial on the facing page: "Some readers undoubtedly will believe that we are getting a wee bit carried away when we turn to sex in order to sell a UFO newspaper.... We really aren't trying to capture a larger audience by printing a sensationalistic headline on our cover. If we wanted to take this approach, we'd do what the other saucer publications so frequently do—simply fabricate the stories we print. But we don't cater to the gullible. We take our work here at *UFO Review* quite seriously. All the items we mention in our story are fully documented. We need not substitute fiction for truth—for truth is far greater than fiction in the field of UFOlogy."

The keystone of Beckley's "saucer sex" story was a newspaper account dated February 12, 1978, entitled "Kidnapped to Venus." Reporter Jerry Burger related how a thirty-one-year-old librarian was found by police as she wandered nude in a town park. She claimed she had been "abducted by Venusians," taken to the "back of the moon," and there "implanted with outer-space semen" before being returned to earth. Beckley reported the case as true and added that "such reports are taking place on a global scale.... There can be little doubt from the documented evidence that some tremendous event is slated to happen that will guide us to a higher understanding of ourselves and the cosmos.... The UFOnauts are trying to teach us a lesson—that love is universal and encompasses every living creature, regardless of their planet or dimension of origin." And for those readers who wanted more information, Beckley added that the "saucer sex" story is just one chapter in his new book, *Strange Encounters—Bizarre & Eerie Contacts with Flying Saucers,* available from the author: $6.95 plus postage and handling.

Unfortunately, Beckley's story is even more absurd than it first appears—and that's saying a lot. Houston spaceflight expert Robert Nichols actually unearthed the original of the newspaper clipping quoted by Beckley. The article did not come from a real newspaper at all, but from a 1978 satirical publication, the *Sunday Newspaper Parody* written by the *National Lampoon*

The ultimate in disputes: Dr. Hynek believes that eleven year old David Dorn, of Lincolnshire, Illinois, had a "true UFO experience" when he took these photographs in 1974; Robert Sheaffer concluded that the case was a crude hoax, and I agree. Photos courtesy CUFOS.

staff. Beckley (or somebody on his staff) evidently made some editorial changes to enhance the credibility (such as it is) of the article, changing the original spelling of the saucer rape victim from the highly suspicious "Penelope Cuntz" to the acceptably ethnic "Penelope Kuntz," and altering the name of the newspaper from the rather utopian Dacron, Ohio *Republican-Democrat* to the Toronto *Sunday Sun.* The entire account, then, is a fictional spoof—but the extent of Beckley's role in promoting it and altering it (or merely passing it along credulously) is still undetermined.

(Beckley steadfastly has refused to admit his mistake, and at one point in 1981 even asserted that the Toronto paper had copied the idea from the *Lampoon,* or else maybe vice versa. But finally James Moseley, who was mediating the dispute in his UFO newsletter, voted for my version, writing that I "had Beckley by the short hairs" whether he 'fessed up or not.)

All UFO accounts are not hoaxes, of course. In fact, only a tiny percentage of raw UFO reports turn out to be hoaxes. However, the overwhelming majority of all published UFO photographs are hoaxes—either forgeries, models, or misrepresented ordinary phenomena (as even UFO proponents generally acknowledge).

A classic UFO photographic hoax involved the "Fogl flying saucer" pictures, taken in December 1957 and first published in 1959. As chronicled by skeptical UFOlogist David A. Schroth, the photographs were embraced by magazines in Britain and America; UFO experts argued that some features on the bottom of the flying saucer were identical to features seen in other photographs, testifying to the authenticity of Fogl's photographs. American UFO publicist Ray Palmer declared, "We are forced to admit this is not a fake...." In 1966, one of the photographs was presented as authentic in *Life.*

That may have been the last straw for Fogl, who later that year finally revealed that the photographs were faked—they were made with a small model hung on a wire. When asked why he did it, Fogl replied that he wanted to show "that certain people make utter fools of themselves. Far too many people make a racket of the UFO business—writing phony books supported by faked pictures."

As if in fulfillment of Fogl's point, many UFO writers continued to use the hoax pictures. Ray Palmer (who is credited by UFO historian Daniel Cohen as having "invented" the concept of "flying saucers") wrote that it was "impossible" for the photos to be fakes and that Fogl's confession must be a hoax. And in 1979

Computer enhancement revealed the string holding up the model in this famous
Spanish "UMMO" UFO hoax. Courtesy GEPAN & GSW.

McGraw-Hill published David C. Knight's *UFOs: A Pictorial History,* with page 86 proudly presenting one of the Fogl pictures as still authenticated!

UFO hoaxes continue to be written up as "authentic" in the media long after they have been publicly discredited.

As part of a "UFO flap" in 1897, the story of Alexander Hamilton of Yates Center, Kansas, stands out. The farmer reported that a cigar-shaped airship flown by jabbering humanoids had hovered over his farm and had caught hold of a calf with a rope. His account was published in the local newspaper along with a statement vouching for his honesty, signed by five leading citizens of the town. The story rapidly spread around the world—and for decades, UFO writers considered it one of the best documented "Close Encounters of the Third Kind" ever. Jacques Vallee endorsed it firmly.

Hamilton and the five leading citizens actually had organized a loal "Liars Club" and Hamilton's "calfnapping airship" whopper, a tall tale through and through, topped all the other attempts. The newspaper story was all a joke, as it turned out, but neither the editor nor the town citizens realized how seriously the outside world had taken the account. It was not until early 1977 that the full story appeared, in *FATE* magazine. Associate Editor Jerry Clark, a diligent and highly-principled pro-UFO investigator, revealed what he called "the biggest hoax ever known in UFO history" when he published hitherto-unknown documentation (found by Robert Schadewald) which established beyond a shadow of a doubt that the Hamilton story was phony.

But the same old UFOric pattern continued. New writers based their books and articles on older UFO books and articles, not on original sources or independent verification. Among the subsequent UFO literature which continued to use the Hamilton story as if it were authentic were Knight's *UFOs: A Pictorial History* and the *Ripley's Believe it or Not: Stars, Space and UFOs* (33rd in a series)—but at least in this latter case, the readers were given the option of believing or not!

Once in a while, though, a UFO hoax does get scotched before it grows big enough to become widely reported and accepted.

The January 1980 issue of the *UFO Journal* (issued by MUFON, the "Mutual UFO Network," a well-organized private research group with a good reputation) provides one such case, as well as some very interesting insights into the minds of a UFO hoaxer and of the UFO investigator who worked on the case.

The witness was a twenty-six-year-old security guard who claimed to have encountered space aliens (as opposed to the more

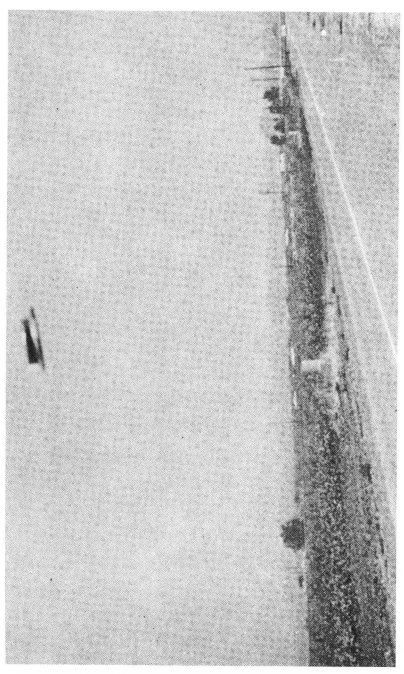

The "Rex Heflin Photos" are disputed even between UFO groups; skeptics believe
the "flying saucer" is hanging from a pole outside the witness's truck's windshield.

common illegal aliens) in the San Joaquin valley in 1977. A year and a half later, after trying to dig up supporting evidence, he contacted MUFON.

The investigator (who, along with the witness, was kept anonymous in the article) reported that "I was impressed with this young man's sincerity, his apparent honesty, and his concern that he was unable to locate any other witnesses. I am by nature a cautious and suspicious person...having run into enough hoaxes and fraudulent cases in my twenty-two years of investigation to give me adequate insight and recognition for such incidents...I was quite satisfied as to his honesty."

But at the end of the article, the entire tone changed: "The important message for all of us," wrote editor Richard Hall, "is that this case is a hoax—a confessed hoax." The investigators didn't find this out for sure until the article had been typeset, but they decided to publish it anyway as a lesson in human vulnerability to hoaxes: "The story content fit so well with other cases, and the reporter seemed so 'sincere' and in a responsible position, that we were nearly taken in."

Even without the confession, MUFON investigators had become suspicious of glaring discrepancies in the story as told to different investigators—but even those factors might not have been enough to prove the case a hoax if the witness himself had not confessed when confronted with the inconsistencies and contradictions in his own story.

In a letter to MUFON, the hoaxer (code-named "Carl" to preserve his anonymity) explained his motives: "All my life I had been a nobody, unimportant...I wanted to be important...I am not psychologically deranged but just wanted some attention." But he had not seemed to act as if he sought attention—he certainly had not sought publicity. Indeed, the investigator had originally reported that "fearing ridicule and harassment from friends and co-workers, Carl kept this story to himself until he simply had to tell someone who would help ease his frustration and anxiety." Evidently the "adequate insight" into hoaxes which the MUFON investigator claimed to possess was inadequate.

MUFON's decision to publish the San Joaquin hoax story with the confession was a courageous one since it did make its investigator sound rather foolish. But the UFO group demonstrated commendable maturity in choosing to try to have all its investigators learn from the experience—lest such incidents be repeated on a wide scale.

Monteleone's space trip to Lanulos was not universally swallowed, either. It was never believed by most of the "nuts and

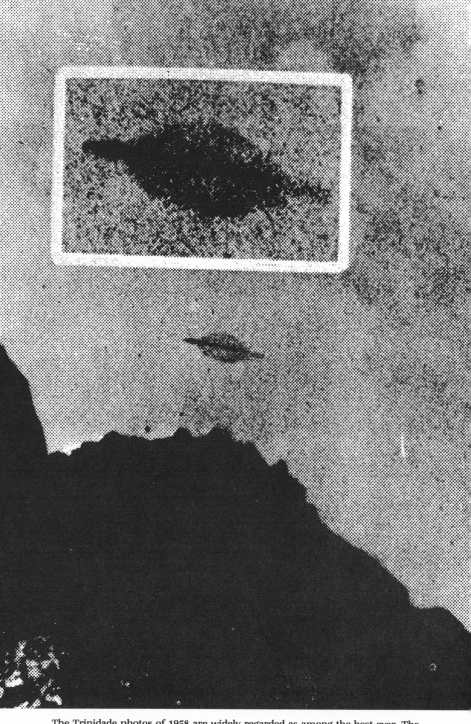

The Trinidade photos of 1958 are widely regarded as among the best ever. The witness was a professional trick photographer and Donald Menzel has argued persuasively that this is a hoax.

bolts" UFO buffs who have for decades despised crackpot contactees and the bad publicity they have brought to the movement. UFOlogical observer James Moseley, editor of *Flying Saucer News,* had written that Monteleone clearly was not a "classic contactee" and evidently never believed his own story—a perceptive conclusion. And, the fake Fogl photographs and Simpson Warminster experiment-hoax would probably not have survived the sophisticated photo-analytic techniques now used by some UFO groups (notably William Spaulding's high-technology "Ground Saucer Watch" in Phoenix.)

The extent to which serious UFO groups now seem determined to detect and reject hoaxes was demonstrated in 1980 when—practically without exception—all major groups and leading investigators publicly denounced the Genesis-III Productions' photo book *UFOs: Contact from the Pleiades.* While the strikingly handsome collection of flying saucer photographs was being billed by its publishers as the greatest UFO breakthrough in human history, a number of pro-UFO researchers circulated reports which claimed that the whole business was a money-making fraud. For once, UFO skeptics agreed with their traditionally antagonistic pro-UFO counterparts.

UFO skeptics, however, go even further in their accusations of "hoax!" and find themselves in bitter disagreement with pro-UFO forces. Some of the highly-publicized classic UFO encounters (such as the 1973 Pascagoula fishermen's account and the 1975 Snowflake, Arizona woodcutters' account) and some of the classic UFO photographs (such as the 1950 McMinnville photos and the 1957 Trinidade Island photos) are considered by skeptics to be hoaxes. Half of the "best UFO cases" of the 1970s—as judged by a "Blue Ribbon Panel" of UFO experts sponsored by the *National Enquirer*—are considered hoaxes, according to independent research by skeptics. Here the battle lines are clearly drawn.

Suggesting that a UFO case is a hoax poses delicate problems. First of all, the UFO witness (whether a hoaxer or not) may have grounds for a libel lawsuit—but although many threats along these lines have been made, so far none have been filed. Secondly, without a confession it is extremely difficult to actually *prove* an accusation of "hoax"—however suspicious the story may sound. Lastly, UFO skeptics (in particular, the world's undisputed leading skeptic, aviation journalist Philip J. Klass) open themselves up to countercharges of "character assassination" and "vicious *ad hominem* attacks" when they point out—

usually quite correctly—that the reliability of many famous UFO witnesses is highly questionable due to their past and subsequent histories of exaggeration, fantasy, and outright deception (pro-UFO groups generally downplay or even cover up such behavior on the part of people whose credibility they wish to emphasize).

Despite the problems caused by UFO hoaxes (mainly, that they can be far more difficult to solve or even recognize than are "ordinary" honest UFO reports), these patterns in deception can be made useful. Successful hoaxes can help calibrate the reliability of UFO research, as in the case of Monteleone's and Simpson's hoaxes; hoaxes can also instruct serious investigators in caution and humility, as with the San Joaquin hoax reported in the MUFON *UFO Journal.*

The claim of the super-skeptics—that unsolved UFO cases can all easily be dismissed as unrecognized hoaxes—is unsubstantiated; the claim of UFO eager-believers—that the hoax problem is under control—is equally unsubstantiated, if not refuted. The dilemma continues.

Note: If any readers have ever participated in a successful UFO hoax—or if they know of anyone who has—and they wish to report this accomplishment to *OMNI* for possible publication, they can contact this columnist directly. There's no law against UFO hoaxes, even those that received cash prizes, while as this article shows, ultimately-revealed UFO hoaxes are extremely valuable for improving UFO research. And a revelation of a successful UFO hoax, with the full account of how it was conceived and executed and swallowed, is likely to bring more and better publicity and recognition to its perpetuator than did the original hoax. So please help out if you can.

PART TWO
Outer Space Mysteries

CHAPTER SIX
The Sirius Mystery

The search for an extraterrestrial calling card has taken researchers to many strange places. Some have hiked the Andes to examine mysterious ruins while others have sought alien traces in deserts and jungles. Others have scoured the rare book rooms in libraries and pored over dusty volumes of Mesopotamian or Sanskrit legend. Some have analyzed UFO reports, others have tried to puzzle out the source and meaning of baffling long-delayed radio echoes.

Several specialists now claim they have found the long-sought "final evidence" of visits made to earth by ancient astronauts. The myths of the Dogon tribesmen of Mali, West Africa, contain astronomical knowledge which the native people could have neither learned by themselves nor guessed. Obviously, the researchers say, some more advanced civilization told them.

These fascinating Dogon legends speak of Jupiter's four moons and Saturn's rings, which were not seen by human beings until the invention of the telescope. They speak of the star Sirius and of a pair of invisible companions. One of them circles Sirius every fifty years, the legends declare, and is made of a metal that is the heaviest thing in the universe. Astronomers have discovered that such an object (called "Sirius-B") does exist but only the most sophisticated and sensitive instruments—unavailable, of course, to the Dogons—can detect it.

The planets circle the sun, the tribesmen believe (and astronomy confirms), in elliptical orbits. And planets with different kinds of people on them circle six other stars in the sky—so the legends have it.

Who told the Dogons about Sirius and about the other space science secrets? Author Robert K. G. Temple (*The Sirius Mystery*, St. Martin's Press, 1975) claims to be able to trace the Sirius-B myth back through Egyptian mythology to Sumerian mythology, thus establishing the certainty that the informants were extraterrestrials. Ancient astronauts entrepreneur Erich von Daniken endorses and adopts Temple's explanations in his latest book, *Von Daniken's Proof*.

But other observers disagree. Astronomers Carl Sagan and Ian Ridpath, for example, have suggested that the modern astronomical aspects of the complex Dogon mythology entered the lore only recently, probably shortly before the myths were written down in the 1930s. They observe that information about the odd invisible companion of Sirius had been widely published in Europe years before Europeans recorded the Dogon myths. As anthropologists have known for a long time, primitive tribes have a remarkable talent for absorbing interesting new stories into their traditional mythology.

In reply Temple produces evidence for the great antiquity of the Sirius cult. The number "fifty" has great signifance in ancient myths. He points out that the Dogon myths also describe a third star (astronomers would call it "Sirius C"), as yet undiscovered. These same myths, Temple claims, identify a planet circling that star as the home of Nommo, an alien creature who founded the Dogon civilization.

Temple's impressive research was encouraged by noted futurist Arthur C. Clarke (although Clarke now prefers the "modern influence" hypothesis). The book's advertising blurb quotes prolific science writer Isaac Asimov, who says, "I couldn't find any mistakes in this book. That in itself is extraordinary."

The star Sirius is certainly no stranger to mysteries. As the brightest star in the sky it was known and worshiped by ancient civilizations. Its appearance in the dawn sky over Egypt warned of the impending Nile floods and the summer's heat and marked the beginning of the Egyptian calendar.

Strangely, ancient records explicitly list Sirius as one of six "red stars." The other five are still seen as red but from the time of Arab astronomers to the present day Sirius has been blue-white.

Astronomers classify Sirius as a "class A" star, hotter and

younger than our sun. Its brightness is due largely to its proximity; it is barely eight light-years away from the earth. This is only a stellar stone's throw by galactic standards and Sirius is only twice as far away from our solar system as are the nearest stars to the sun, the Alpha Centauri system.

Sirius figures prominently in the Dogon myths. The tribe has a periodic Sirius festival called the "Segui" ceremony; each celebration lasts several years (the last was in 1968-72.) The interval between ceremonies may be forty, fifty or sixty years.

Through the carbon dating of old ritual masks researchers have established the antiquity of the Segui ceremonies. Such criteria suggest that these periodic festivals have been going on for at least 600 years and possibly much longer.

But here's the rub: there is no archaeological evidence that the specific references to the twin hidden companions of Sirius are anywhere near that old. Furthermore, most Dogon symbology already has multiple levels of meaning; the sketches used to illustrate the Sirius secrets are also used in puberty ceremonies. Clearly the Dogons (in common with many other cultures) were fascinated by Sirius, probably because its position in the sky was crucial to successful agriculture (it's the only star they have a name for.) Inevitably one must ask, if the Dogons had heard good stories about Sirius from other sources, would they ignore them or would they quickly adopt them into their own cultural myths?

Temple's book mentions the absorption of a Christ-figure into the traditional Dogon Pantheon, obviously a recent addition. Sagan has recounted numerous examples from Arizona and New Guinea—and other scholars have noted similar instances—of the rapid assimilation of new stories, songs and lore into the eclectic mythology of Stone Age peoples. Such assimilation occurs most frequently when the subject is one of particular interest to a people—as Sirius is to the Dogons.

The main problem with the alleged antiquity of the Dogon "Sirius secrets" legend is that they are reminiscent of European Sirius speculations of the late 1920s. Europeans too believed that the "white dwarf" Sirius-B star was the heaviest thing in the universe, although in later years astronomers were to find thousands of similar objects along with even heavier and denser objects such as neutron stars and black holes. Europeans too talked about the discovery of a third star in the Sirius system; later investigations, however, ruled out that possibility.

The Dogon beliefs about Jupiter and Saturn sound familiar too. To be specific they sound like the kinds of astronomical conclusions one might draw from studying the heavens through a small portable telescope. (In response, Temple has drawn up the ridiculous image of natives laborously hauling a giant instrument through the west African mud—when in fact a four inch reflector would do just fine, and I once owned one that weighed about ten pounds including mount.) The Dogons hold that Jupiter has four moons when in fact it has at least 12, plus a ring, as any true extraterrestrial would have known. Saturn is not, as the Dogons insist, the farthest planet in the solar system. At least three are farther and at least one of them has rings too.

So what is the alternative to the extraterrestrial hypothesis for the Dogon myths? The Dogons could have learned of European Sirius lore in the 1920's from traders, explorers or missionaries, many of whom are avid amateur astronomers. (Temple claims missionaries didn't show up until 1949.) The Dogons were not isolated. Many served in the French army in World War I and some of them could have returned years later with colorful embellishments for their native legends.

But the extraterrestrial hypothesis will not fade away so easily. Robert Temple, who spent eight years studying mythology, is convinced that he can trace the Sirius-B information back to the Sumerians. This of course would destroy the modern influence explanation totally.

Unfortunately the ancient records contain no clear, unambiguous references to this Sirius lore although the works of historians, astronomers and philosophers were explicit and detailed on innumerable other subjects. But that doesn't stop Temple. He says the references *are* there but recorded in riddles which he alone has been able to decipher. "The ancient peoples were not concealing information from us out of spite," he writes. "Their purpose in disguising their secrets was to see that the secrets could survive."

To penetrate this supposed disguise (which might not be a disguise at all, other classical scholars maintain), Temple resorts to ancient puns, to hidden meanings, to "garbled versions" which he must amend to fit the theory, to the exchange of consonants in innocent-looking words, to similar-sounding words from different civilizations thousands of miles or thousands of years apart and to other equally questionable tactics.

Using similar techniques other writers have "discovered" dozens of different, often contradictory "ancient secrets" about Atlantis, primitive Christianity, forgotten wisdom, ancient visitors and numerous other things. Classical mythology has been a Rorschach test into which people have projected nearly any notion that appealed to them. We need more reliable evidence—especially theories that can be tested.

Temple has made very few verifiable assertions about mythology (and *The Sirius Mystery* is overwhelmingly about ancient myths, not about the Dogons or modern astronomy). One such rare claim is that "the oasis (Siwa) and Thebes are both equidistant from Behdet . . . (This proves that) geodetic surveys of immense accuracy were thus practiced in ancient Egypt with a knowledge of the earth as a spherical body in space and projections upon it envisaged as part of . . . the Sirius lore." This sounds significant and convincing until one measures the distance on a map and discovers an "immensely accurate equality" of a twenty percent difference! Other Temple claims, including some wild assertions from *The Secrets of the Great Pyramid,* can as easily be checked and as easily demolished.

But didn't Isaac Asimov check over the book for just such factual errors, as the publisher claims? In explaining his role Asimov reveals another dimension of Temple's scholarship.

"Robert Temple on three different occasions, by mail and phone, attempted to get support from me and I steadfastly refused," Asimov wrote. "He sent me the manuscript which I found unreadable. Finally, he asked me point-blank if I could point out any errors in it and partly out of politeness, partly to get rid of him, and partly because I had been able to read very little of the book so that the answer was true, I said I could not point out any errors. He certainly did not have permission to use that statement as part of the promotion. I'll just have to be even more careful hereafter."

Temple's book is indeed extremely long and many other researchers have echoed Asimov's assertion that it is "unreadable." But was anything left out?

The author mentions that he could have made the book much longer but restrained himself "lest I blow this book up into a puffball of miscellaneous odds and ends"—which prompted one reviewer to remark that Temple had stopped much too late to avoid that fate.

But even after hundreds of pages of myths and interpretations Temple fails to make a connection between ancient Egypt and the modern Dogons; instead he "assumes" it. Nor does he establish a connection between the Dogon creator Nommo and the star Sirius. Temple claims that bas-reliefs of the Sumerian demigod Oannes, which depict a "fish man," prove Nommo, whom the author identifies as the ancestor of the Dogon Nommo myths, was an amphibious extraterrestrial. Unfortunately he neglects to mention other bas-reliefs which show "fish-deer" and "fish-lions" and which consequently suggest that the fish motif was symbolic, not descriptive.

Somehow, Temple and I have never gotten our disputes off on the right foot. When I set him a draft of a sharply critical review written for *Astronomy* magazine, he replied with a blistering counterattack in a letter to my editor: "A virulent attack against my honesty, integrity, and intelligence," he called my review. "Mr. Oberg has entirely misrepresented me and made violent distortions of my argument.... He shows a total ignorance or disregard for almost every fact in my book, and there is hardly a single thing in his review which is remotely accurate." The review was indeed consequently modified in parts where Temple explained portions of his book I may have misinterpreted.

Here is an example of how hard it can be to critically examine the claims in the book. There is one passage (page 65) which I took to mean implied additional confirmation of Temple's hypothetical aquatic inhabitants of the Sirius system: "It is worth pointing out that in the event of planets in the Sirius system being watery, we must seriously consider the possibility of intelligent beings from there being amphibious....Beings of this type would be a bit like mermaids and mermen....Perhaps the 'sirens' are, figuratively, a chorus of mermaids recalled from earlier times....They are called in Greek *Seiren*....It is interesting that the Greek Sirius is *Seirios*."

I assumed, reasonably I believe, that Temple meant to prove something by this chain of development, and I said it was a silly idea. In a response published in *Fate* magazine, he denied intending that: "I refer, entirely in passing, to the Greek word for siren and its similarity to the word for Sirius, drawing absolutely no conclusions of any kind." If so, I wonder why that passage was ever "worth pointing out" in the book in the first place.

Another claim: that in Egypt the oasis of Siwa and the ancient Nile City of Thebes are both equidistant from the shrine city of Behdet, in the delta—and the same exact distance, too. To Temple, this proved that "geodetic surveys of immense accuracy were thus practiced in ancient Egypt with a knowledge of the earth as a spherical body in space and projections upon it envisaged as part of...the Sirius lore." (And presumably, that the Egyptians then located their river deltas, oases, and river ports deliberately on geometric rather than purely geographical grounds, I'm tempted to ask?) But my own measurements, which I published, showed the distances to be nowhere close, in error by tens of miles, at least ten percent—hardly "immense accuracy."

Temple replied in *Fate*: "The pattern published in my book was drawn by a professional cartographer who earns his living by drawing reliable maps for an international corporation." He allegedly found the distances "to be nearly equal to one another"—although no quantitative definition of "nearly equal" was ever offered. "Perhaps [Oberg] is unaware," Temple went on, "that the differential curvature of the earth variously distorts distances shown on maps. The cartographer took all such factors into account. Did Oberg? I suspect not."

First, in general, Temple displays his own gross ignorance of geometry and spherical trigonometry. At the latitude of Egypt, over distances of several hundred kilometers, planetary curvature introduces distortions only on the order of fractions of kilometers, not the tens of kilometers worth of innaccuracies I found in Temple's claim.

Second, while it is difficult to obtain precise locations of many archeological sites referred to in the *Sirius Mystery*, Temple himself shows a map that gives the location of Behdet (31.23 °E, 31.50 °N) and Thebes (32.63 °E, 25.70 °N). For Siwa, I called Dr. Farouk El-Baz of the National Air and Space Museum in Washington, and his maps showed it at 25.50 °E, 29.22 °N (that's the oasis center, with the modern town about ten kilometers SE).

So it merely remains for any interested reader to check and see which of us is correct. Using spherical trig, I got 612.3 km for the Siwa-Behdet leg and 654.8 km for the Thebes-Behdet. Temple *claims* his expert cartographer found these distances "nearly equal." I wonder.

One additional disturbing note: That distance has been computed based on a true geodetic oblate spheroid, but even assuming a flat surface would only have introduced an error of a few tenths of one percent at most (Temple obviously didn't know that, or he wouldn't have asserted that measurements even less accurate than that were proof that ancients took Earth's sphericity into account.) The greatest source of error, however, seems to be in Temple's specified location of Behdet. Precise maps at the NASA space photo interpretation lab in Houston list "Behdet" as an ancient name for modern Damanhur, located today at 31.03 °N, 30.28 °E, i.e., more than a hundred kilometers away from where Temple locates his "Behdet" at 31.50 °N, 31.23 °E. Damanhur is 521.0 km from Siwa and 625.9 km from Thebes, a deviation of 20%.

Am I getting too picky here? Perhaps so—it does seem like a trivial point, arguing over how different two meaningless geographical distances really are. There are innocent available explanations: typographical error or miscopied notes, for example. But if the error is real, it reflects on the only kind of hard, checkable, testable evidence Temple has offered for his theories. A critical analysis has to investigate the accuracy of such claims, so as to judge the validity of the book's conclusions.

Temple offered another line of reasoning. "We have in the Dogon information a predictive mechanism which it is our duty to test, regardless of our preconceptions." One example: "If a Sirius-C is ever discovered and found to be a red dwarf, I will conclude that the Dogon information has been fully validated." (OK, I'll bite—but if such a star is not discovered, Temple has risked no converse conclusions.) Another example: "The Dogon also mention a period of rotation of Sirius-B...one year...this rotation is astronomically possible but whether it is correct or not we cannot yet know. Here, then, is another datum to be investigated when it is possible." (OK, but if it's not true then Temple may suddenly discover that, as in another similar case, "the Dogon information...must be not only garbled (or perhaps concealed in line with a secretive tradition) but only partially true."—in other words, no disproof would follow the failure of his prediction.)

That's one major characteristic of classical pseudo-science, its ability to incorporate *any* result and its ability to be immune from disproof from any result. Predictions are often reinterpreted to fit any outcome, which makes them scientifically worthless but which can be claimed to verify the pseudo-scientific claims.

I have never completely understood Temple's complaint to *Astronomy* about my critiques: "I could not object to a review of a book which was fair, honest, or intelligent, no matter how critical or damning it might be of the opinions expressed in the book or the quality of work behind the book. But it is an unfortunate tendency for certain reviewers to wish to try and appear clever at the expense of accuracy, honesty, objectivity, fairness, or even decent manners, by dropping any standards at all in their headlong assaults on authors using only the tools of distortion, dishonesty, and insults. And this is what Mr. Oberg has done." Whew! (I must confess *I've* felt that way about some *other* people, too!).

Such words would have more persuasion behind them (to me they're merely an emotional appeal to sympathy) *if* Temple had ever admitted anywhere in print that he had found (or had been shown) any errors in his book or articles or public statements—but if he has done so, I haven't become aware of them.

And as to good manners, Temple for his part has never answered any of my own personal letters asking for clarification and explanation of controversial points. Instead, he closed his response to my own article in 1979 with a brushoff: "In my view it is pointless to attack someone in print unless you can substantiate what you are saying. Since Oberg cannot do so, we need not concern ourselves with criticisms of *The Sirius Mystery.*" I certainly concur with the first of those sentences!

If I were alone in picking on Temple's thesis, he might be able to argue a case for *ad hominem* persecution. But other observers have also written skeptically about the "Sirius Mystery."

A series of articles has appeared in the *Griffith Observer,* an astronomy magazine issued monthly by the Griffith Observatory in Los Angeles. September 1976 saw Tom Sever's "The Obsession with the Star Sirius," and editor Ron Oriti's "On Not Taking it Seriously." October 1977 saw Marvin Luckermann's "More Sirius Difficulties," on ancient calendar systems and an alternate, non-extraterrestrial explanation for the ancient fascination with the number fifty (the article quotes Michael Astour's book *Hellenosemitics* as saying, "This exorbitant figure, very popular in Greek myths, has its explanation: it is the number of seven-day weeks in one lunar year. The proof is supplied by (the *Odyssey),* where Helios is said to possess 7 herds of 50 cows each and 7 herds of 50 sheep, a transparent allegory of the days and nights of the year.") In September 1980, Dr. Philip C. Steffey did an in-depth analysis of Dogon astronomical traditions in "Some Serious Astronomy in the 'Sirius Mystery,' " which criticized Temple's book as "inadequate and full of factual errors and misrepresentation of critical material."

British astronomy popularizer Ian Ridpath, writing in the quarterly *Skeptical Inquirer* (Fall 1978), blasted Temple's "brain-numbing excursions into Egyptology." The Dogon legend connected with Sirius, wrote Ridpath, "is riddled with ambiguities, contradictions, and downright errors, at least if we try to interpret it literally." And does the Dogon mythology ever really say that Nommo, the founder of their culture, came from Sirius—which is at the crux of Temple's reconstruction? "It does not!" Ridpath asserts. "Nowhere in his 290-page book does Temple offer one specific statement from the Dogon to substantiate his ancient astronauts claim." Concluded Ridpath: "The parts of the Dogon knowledge that are admittedly both ancient and profound, particularly the story of Nommo and the concept of twinning, are the parts that bear least relation to the true facts about Sirius. The parts that bear at least a superficial resemblance to astronomical facts are most likely trimmings added in this century. Indeed, in view of the Dogon fixation with Sirius it would surely be more surprising if they had *not* grafted on to their existing legend some new astronomical information gained from Europeans....We may never be able to reconstruct the exact route by which the Dogon received their current knowledge, but out of the confusion at least one thing is clear: they were not told by beings from the star Sirius."

Carl Sagan's contribution to this discussion was in his book *Broca's Brain* (1979). "At first glance," Sagan admitted, "the Sirius legend of the Dogon seems to be the best candidate evidence available today for man's past contact with advanced extraterrestrial civilization." But Sagan then finds both astronomical and mythological holes in the hypothesis. "There is some evidence," he points out, "that the Dogon like to frame pictures with an ellipse, and that Temple may be mistaken about the claim that in Dogon mythology the planets and Sirius-B move in elliptical orbits." Further, "The fact that the Dogon do not talk of another planet with rings beyond Saturn [i.e., Uranus, whose rings were discovered in 1977—and the rings of Jupiter weren't discovered until after Sagan's book was written, although they would have been clearly visible to any arriving extraterrestrial spacecraft] suggests to me that their informants were European, not extraterrestrial." Concludes Sagan, "There are too many loopholes, too many alternate explanations for such a myth to provide reliable evidence of past extraterrestrial contact."

Nevertheless the Sumerian Oannes myths, first described by Sagan and Shklovskiy in *Intelligent Life in the Universe* in 1966, are as intriguing as ever. In a recent book, *The Once and Future Star* (Hawthorn Books, 1977), George Michanowsky identifies "Oannes" as a Hellenized version of the Sumerian name Ea; he theorizes that the myths may refer to a gigantic supernova. Modern astronomers have discovered the remains of the supernova Vela-X in a constellation which would have been visible in the low southern sky from Sumer.

The mystery of the ancient "red" Sirius also remains baffling. Some astronomers speculate that the white dwarf Sirius B might have been a flaming red giant only 2000 years ago although current astrophysical theories decree that any such transformation in less than 100,000 years is impossible. Other ancient astronomical records make no mention of Sirius being red.

Meanwhile the Dogon myths continue to baffle investigators.

The obviously advanced astronomical knowledge must have come from somewhere, but is it an ancient bequest or a modern graft? Although Temple fails to prove its antiquity, the evidence for the recent acquisition of the information is still entirely circumstantial.

Dogon descriptions of Jupiter, Saturn and Sirius remind one of Jonathan Swift's uncanny description of the two undiscovered moons of Mars. But that isn't the only parallel. Swift appears to have taken the idea of two close (although not necessarily small) moons of Mars from Voltaire's novel *Micromegas* in which an extraterrestrial visitor tells earthmen about the undiscovered Martian moons. And from what star system does the visitor come? You quessed it—Sirius!

In 1977 two radio astronomers were interested enough in the Sirius mystery to direct their telescopes at the star system in hopes of picking up any artificial radio signals. None were detected. That was not surprising since, judging from the age and energy of the stars in the Sirius system, astronomers believe it is unlikely that any earthlike planets could exist there long enough for life to emerge and develop.

So where does this leave the mysteries of Sirius? The antiquity of the Dogon astronomy is not so obvious as ancient astronaut enthusiasts claim but neither has it been disproved. The ancient records are filled with unanswered astronomical questions—including the "red Sirius" and the possible Sumerian Ea-Oannes references to the spectacular Vela-X supernova. The Dogon myths may or may not be related to these other puzzles (or even to Kepler's supernova, which has been seriously suggested.) It seems likely that we will never know for sure.

Whatever their place in the search for extraterrestrial contact, the Dogon myths are certainly odd. The Stone Age storytellers speak by their campfires of other people on other planets and of other mysteries. Our mysteries may be different but our questions are the same and we are no wiser.

Chapter Seven
The Tunguska Echoes

A mighty midair explosion over a remote Siberian swamp is still sending echoes around the world, seven decades after it happened. Near the Tunguska River, in the summer of 1908, an object from outer space was annihilated in a detonation as powerful as a modern hydrogen bomb. If the object was a natural one, it serves as a warning of a repeated disaster over a populated region today; if the object was not natural, it serves as an interplanetary calling card, announcing to those who can recognize and decipher it that an attempt had been made at interplanetary contact.

The "Tunguska Event" remains a puzzle for science, even as it has become a fertile subject for science fiction and UFO speculation. Recently, two TV drama critics, Thomas Atkins and John Baxter, threw together a book called *The Fire Came By* (Doubleday, 1976, condensed in the February 1978 *Reader's Digest*), which insists that the only possible explanation for the event is that it was an exploding nuclear-powered interstellar spaceship. Soviet scientist Aleksey Zolotov makes the world news wires about once a year with a new version of his claim to have discovered radioactivity at the impact site. The flying-saucer subculture has firmly canonized the Tunguska Event as physical proof of UFOs.

Not surprisingly, traditional astronomers reject that interpretation as fanciful and unscientific, as "not required," and

132

as insufficient. The leading standard theory for the twenty-megaton (equivalent to twenty million tons of TNT) explosion is that it was a comet nucleus that exploded upon hitting the earth's atmosphere.

It is a first-rate scientific puzzle. Its uncertainties and mysteries provide plenty of dark corners in which all manner of far-out theories can safely lurk. And it is an excellent case study in how different schools of thought use and abuse facts.

So let's look at the Tunguska Event the way it is being reported (and exploited) today and the way it is being scientifically researched. Let's examine the media standards that have been used to inform or misinform the public about this puzzle.

At about 7:15 a.m. local time on June 22, 1908, hundreds of Russian settlers and Tungus natives in the forested hills northwest of Lake Baykal looked up in amazement. A brilliant white light was racing across the sky, casting shadows on the ground, and dazzling the eyes of many who tried to stare at it. Minutes after it passed, a distant rolling thunder came to the ears of the witnesses.

Witnesses twenty to forty miles from the impact point experienced a sudden thermal blast that could be felt through several layers of clothing. For several seconds, half of the sky lit up like a hundred suns. A few moments after the flash, the shock wave arrived, a crashing boom that broke windows and knocked people off their feet.

The blast was recorded as an earthquake at several weather stations in Siberia, and the atmospheric shock wave bounced barograph needles in weather stations in western Europe. A forest fire was ignited that burned for days over several square miles of pine forest.

At sunset that day, the inhabitants of northern Europe were treated to a celestial spectacle that puzzled them for many years. It did not get dark that night. The night sky glowed with an eerie light, and at midnight it was possible to read a newspaper or to photograph the landscape. American observatories later noted that the atmospheric transparency was degraded for several months.

There are third-hand reports of an expedition reaching the site within a year, but all records were destroyed in the bloody civil wars which followed the Bolshevik revolution. It took twenty years for the next scientific teams to reach the point of impact of what was thought to have been a giant meteorite fall (the expedition was financed by the promise that tons of meteoric

The popular "exploding spaceship" theory originated in Russia in 1945. Credit: Griffith Observatory

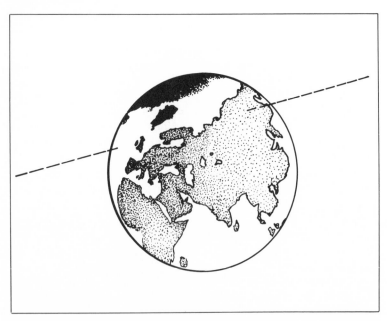

One imaginative hypothesis involved a theoretical "mini-black hole" passing right through the planet. Various problems (including lack of evidence for an exit hole blast) led to the abandonment of the hypothesis by its originators. Credit: Griffith Observatory

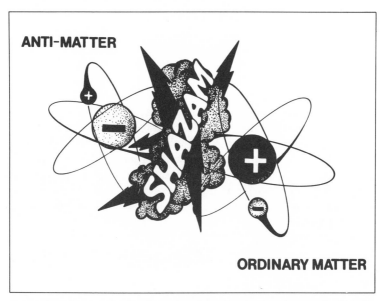

ANTI-MATTER

ORDINARY MATTER

Some physicists toyed with the notion that a hunk of anti-matter had hit the earth—but there wasn't enough residual radioactivity. Credit: Griffith Observatory

The theory of an exploding carbonaceaous comet nucleus has been gaining strength in recent years. Credit: Griffith Observatory

iron would be available for Soviet industry). But no crater could be found. Instead, it was discovered that the trees for miles around had been blasted—from above. Those nearer "ground zero" were still standing but were stripped of their branches and bark. Those further away were smashed down in a direction away from the center.

Years later, a Russian science-fiction writer named Kazantsev was struck by the similarity of the blast effects at Tunguska to those at Hiroshima, which he visited in 1945. A year later, he wrote a story in which the blast at Tunguska was represented as the result of an exploding nuclear power plant of a spaceship from Mars, which was seeking fresh water from Lake Baykal. Many fictitious elements of Kazantsev's imaginative story have since become confused with the real features of the Tunguska story.

Two other Russians adopted—and adapted—the story. A Moscow junior-college lecturer in astronomy named Feliks Zigel, taking time out from studying flying saucers and the Abominable Snowman, became a spokesman for the "spaceship theory" of Tunguska. Physics professor Aleksey Zolotov organized several college expeditions to the Tunguska site and made a series of announcements of "abnormal radioactivity," followed by embarrassed retractions.

These reports of radioactivity at the Tunguska site still persist, but they seem to be groundless. Only Zolotov can find them. Other expeditions, initially as dedicated as Zolotov to the spaceship theory, concluded in disappointment that there was no abnormal radiation beyond traces of fallout from secret Soviet H-bomb tests. Nor did the anomalous fast growth of trees, often a sign of radioactive exposure, impress a special team from the Soviet Forestry Ministry. They discovered that the faster growth followed the distribution of forest fires set off by the blast, to the exclusion of regions closer to ground zero (and hypothetical radioactivity) that did not happen to catch fire. Accelerated growth is an established effect of forest fires, and the Soviet scientists concluded that this had been the case at Tunguska.

In the West, carbon-14 expert and Nobel laureate Willard Libby reported on results of measurements of tree rings in Arizona. There was a small rise in the carbon-14 level following 1908, to be sure, but it was matched by other erratic ups and downs over the years and could have been a random jump. Libby calculated the force of the blast at Tunguska and the radiation that would have been released had the blast involved thermonuclear reactions. He concluded that the low levels of

The comet, perhaps a fragment of Encke's comet, would have approached Earth out of the sun and hence been difficult to see. Credit: Lunar and Planetary Institute (LPI)

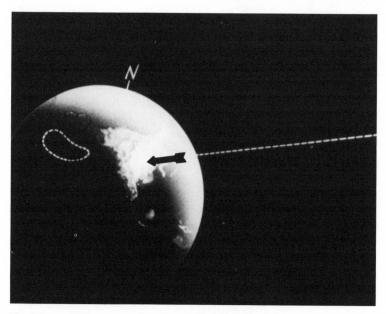

The down-sun dusty tail of the comet would have entered our atmosphere over Northern Europe, where the midsummer midnight sun was just below the northern horizon. Credit: Lunar and Planetary Institute

To examine the blast patterns of crushed trees, Russian scientists set up a "Matchstick forest" and strung explosives above the surface to represent the object's sonic boom and final disintegration. Credit: Lunar and Planetary Institute

In a scene similar to Mt. St. Helens, smashed-down trees covered hundreds of square miles of the region around Tunguska River in Siberia after a mysterious gigantic mid-air blast in 1908.

Insert: Russian explorer Kulik first reached remote site of blast twenty years after the event.

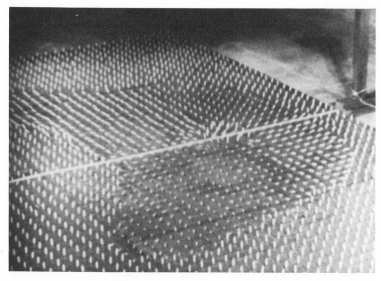

Blast pattern included the characteristic "telephone pole" forest of stripped, standing trees below ground zero. Credit: Lunar and Planetary Institute

carbon-14 he found, even if completely attributable to the blast, could still only count for no more than fifteen percent of the whole force of the detonation. Other carbon-14 tests in Norway, meanwhile, showed absolutely no rise at all following 1908, so these tree-ring experiments are strong evidence that the Tunguska Event did not involve significant nuclear reactions, if any.

But wait a minute! That's not what the modern Tunguska myths tell. Why does the book *UFOs Behind the Iron Curtain*, by Ion Hobana, state explicitly that "Libby is one of the leading proponents of the nuclear theory?" Why does Zolotov still get worldwide attention when he periodically reissues his "discovery" of Tunguska radiation? Why does *The Fire Came By* declare that the thermonuclear nature of the Tunguska blast is inescapable and irrefutable? Why indeed?

In *The Fire Came By,* the spaceship theory has reached its zenith. I had the dubious honor of debating one of the authors on radio a few years ago when the book was being serialized nationwide by the *New York Times.* In the considered opinion of many listeners I "made mincemeat of the poor guy." He hadn't done his homework. He hadn't bothered with contrary evidence and didn't know how to begin to answer it (I had to let him off the hook several times myself, lest the "debate" grind to a halt). He was a TV drama critic who had seen a chance for a successful book, given the right slant and a minimum of responsibility. In terms of its commercial success, he guessed right. Despite friendly words exchanged at the end of the radio debate, he never responded to my letters requesting clarification and support of many of the major claims in the book. His point of view is often expressed in the news media. But I remain willing and eager to reopen the Tunguska debate with the authors or with any other proponent of the spaceship theory in order to get all the facts on record.

So, as a theory, the spaceship hypothesis loses out. Now, follow the arguments for the "comet hypothesis," perhaps not as exciting, but probably a lot more important. Tunguska was not an isolated event; it could happen again, and we better get ready for it.

The "glowing night sky" over Europe was the comet's dust in the upper atmosphere, lit by the midnight sun of the famous midsummer "white nights" (which I have seen from Sweden and Leningrad). An astronomer took a spectrogram and showed that the "eerie glow" was pure reflected sunlight. The comet-earth encounter geometry was such that the object came "out of the sun" and was masked in the daytime sky. Besides, it wasn't a very

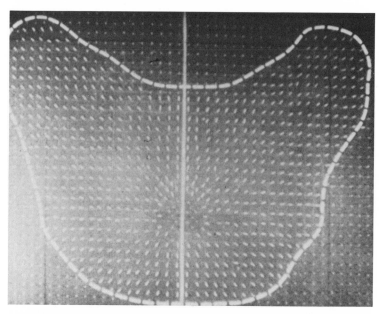

The complete test pattern showed a remarkable resemblance to . . . . Credit: Lunar and Planetary Institute

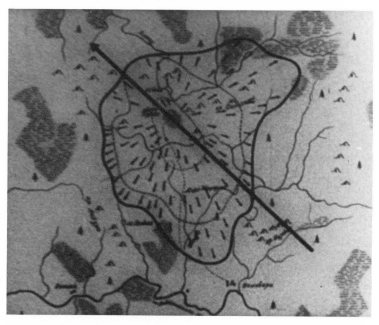

. . . . field surveys of actual smashed-down tree patterns at the Tunguska blast site. Credit: Lunar and Planetary Institute

big comet. (It may have been a hunk of Encke's comet, in fact.) When it hit, the tail was extending "down sun," towards the west, precisely across Europe.

And cometary or meteoric material often does detonate violently on contact with the atmosphere. This is not a chemical or antimatter reaction—it's just the kinetic energy of the speeding object being converted suddenly to tremendous internal heat. Often, only a few hunks of ice and some fine sooty dust will be all that reaches the ground.

Aerodynamics experts in Moscow conducted an experiment about twenty years ago in an effort to simulate Tunguska's blast patterns. The scientists used a charge of explosives suspended over a board covered with miniature "trees" represented by matchsticks. In addition to the single blast point a string of smaller charges were added to reproduce the hypersonic shock wave of the object's ballistic passage through the upper atmosphere.

When the explosives were triggered, a blast pattern strikingly similar to the "butterfly" pattern of the actual Tunguska site was created in the matchstick forest. Although this experiment conclusively demonstrated that the strange pattern was due entirely to a large object that exploded naturally, the experiment's results were still being misinterpreted or misquoted years afterward. According to a 1978 TV program, "The evidence supported the Soviet contention that Tunguska was the result of a nuclear holocaust," a conclusion directly counter to that of the experimenters themselves and a statement that falsely implies that Soviet scientists in general contended that the event was nuclear in origin. They do not.

Meanwhile, every year the "Tunguska UFO" is reborn when some unsuspecting Western newsman in Moscow, searching for an interesting story, falls into the company of Feliks Zigel or Aleksey Zolotov. Within hours, the world's news wires are humming again with an old story that has more lives than the fabled cat: "Top Russian scientists have proved that an atomic UFO crashed in Siberia in 1908."

As more and more evidence piles up indicating that the Tunguska blast was actually caused by a small comet's impact, the handful of "spaceship buffs" seem to have grown more desperate, but no less effective, in corralling the public's attention. Zolotov, for example, has vowed to let his Tolstoyan beard grow until the world adopts his theories. (Needless to say, no professional Soviet geologists or astronomers think much of such tactics or theories.)

Man-made nuclear explosions began in 1945, but the 1908 Tunguska blast had a force equivalent to that of a modern twenty-megaton H-bomb.

Zigel's latest publicity tactics are exemplified in an Associated Press story out of Moscow on October 22, 1978, based on an interview Zigel gave Tass. He boasts that the book *The Fire Came By* independently corroborates his *own* theories, when in fact the authors are actually only quoting Zigel's assertions. Nor are the authors "University of Texas scientists," as the story claims: they are TV drama critics currently enjoying the commercial success of their latest dramatization (some would say fictionalization), while refusing to debate the subject with informed specialists.

Once again, there is no evidence that AP made even the

slightest effort to verify the sensational claims with reputable scientists in the Soviet Union or America. It's an old familiar pattern, and it will take more power than that of the multimegaton Tunguska blast to sweep it away.

The same pattern was replayed on American television recently. Narrating against a background of a man-made nuclear explosion. Leonard Nimoy told viewers of the television documentary "In Search of the Siberian Fireball" that "the evidence now indicates that a nuclear explosion may have occurred on Earth as early as 1908." The show produced by Alan Landsburg Productions and first televised in November, 1978 interviewed some scientists who supported the comet theory, but clearly the program's sympathies were with more exciting suggestions. Thomas Atkins, missing coauthor of *The Fire Came By* (Doubleday 1976) and Henry Gris, coauthor of *The New Soviet Psychic Discoveries* (Prentice Hall, 1978) both argued that an alien spaceship had caused the Tunguska event.

"There is evidence," Atkins wrote, "to indicate that an extraterrestrial vehicle may explain the Siberian explosion. Though the proof is neither complete nor absolutely conclusive, the theory appears increasingly acceptable."

Gris, who refers to the object as the "Tungusky (sic) Miracle," quotes extensively from the testimony of Aleksey Zolotov. He told Gris in Moscow in 1977, "When you hear the descriptions you cannot help forming the opinion that this was no meteorite, but a giant UFO. The explosion (people in the area) saw was a perfect duplicate of what a nuclear blast looks like. . . . Everything points to a nuclear origin. . . . I have no doubt it was sent by inhabitants of outer space to attract our attention."

One selling point for the Baxter-Atkins spaceship book was that the foreword was written by Isaac Asimov. "I found the book fascinating . . . and, in my opinion, worth a hearing," he later wrote in his regular column in *The Magazine of Fantasy and Science Fiction*. But he added a disclaimer: "My friend James Oberg, who has studied the matter closely, thinks I am overgenerous in the opinion, and he may be right."

A most important fact about the craterless mid-air Tunguska blast is that it has happened before and since, at places other than Tunguska. Over western Canada in 1965, a 10-kiloton midair explosion sprinkled meteoric dust over freshly fallen snow, prompting astronomer Ronald Oriti to suggest that the Tunguska Event could have been simply a larger object of the same type. The iconoclastic books of Charles Fort chronicle numerous cases of midair explosions, falling ice, and "black rains." Secret United

States barographic nuclear blast monitors have been picking up strange random explosions in the upper atmosphere several times a year, often of kiloton size or larger. Even a moderate-sized comet air blast today might not be recognized, resulting only in a spate of angry phone calls to the nearest Air Force base. It is possible that many of the "earthquakes" of recorded history, which killed tens of thousands and which leveled cities, may actually have been Tunguska-sized blasts over inhabited areas. The old records must be reread with this new perspective.

This underscores the real danger: there are few uninhabited wastelands on earth today, and even the open sea is covered with human traffic. The records of nature suggest that such giant blasts, or larger ones, can be expected again.

The idea of a Tunguska explosion occurring again, as a human tragedy instead of a scientific (and pseudoscientific) curiosity, is not so far-fetched. But to defend against such future cosmic bombs it is first necessary to recognize them for what they are. Here the spaceship theory and the distortions, omissions, and fabrications of its proponents (both well-meaning and otherwise) remain a major obstacle, and a major danger.

Ultimately, both radar and optical sensors on earth and in space will watch for incoming objects. Missiles based deep in space, armed with multimegaton warheads, will stand guard. Science fiction has long prepared for this scenario, and fact science is now preparing for that eventuality to come to pass. The fictional science and pseudoscience of the "Tunguska spaceship" should be discredited and dismissed as quickly as possible so that we can get on with defending the earth against future "Tunguska comets."

CHAPTER EIGHT

The Mystery of
Russia's Missing Cosmonauts

Everyone seems to like mystery stories with surprise endings. Maybe this is why the Soviet space program is so fascinating to a number of specialists in the U.S. and Europe. The Russians try to hide so much that some things leak out, reminding one of the old proverb that "Nobody has a good enough memory to be a successful liar." Despite the image of impenetrable Soviet secrecy, there are holes in the curtain, and there is a small band of dedicated researchers devoted to peering through these holes.

A good illustration of these efforts is the story of "secret dead Russian cosmonauts" in the early days of the space program. In the absence of concrete information, rumors sprang up from a dozen sources. We were told that Soviet Premier Nikita Khrushchev pounded his shoe at the United Nations in 1960 because his space scientists had just fried several space pilots at the secret Tyuratam space center in Kazakhstan. We heard about radio intercepts from Europe which told of Russian cosmonauts, both men and women, trapped in orbit, slowly dying from suffocation. Lists of these fatal secret missions were compiled, and names, dates, and details of their grisly deaths were put together for more than twenty Russian space phantoms.

But the surprise ending to the mystery was waiting for patient investigators to unravel it. As part of a space history analysis, I spent several months early in 1973 at the Library of

The notorious "Sochi forgery" of a 1961 resort gathering of cosmonauts, from which one man in the back row has been deleted.

Congress in Washington, D.C., cataloguing all the reports of "dead Russian cosmonauts" and comparing them to later revelations such as Khrushchev's memoirs, defectors' tales, and good old-fashioned hindsight. In the process, I solved one set of mysteries—and uncovered another.

It turned out that the rumors we heard twenty years ago (and which still circulate in some publications) were unfounded, and

147

The same man removed from the Sochi photograph was also expunged from a photo on the bus carrying cosmonaut Gagarin to the launch pad (upper left). Behind Gagarin is his spacesuited backup man, Titov; standing are the mystery man (at left) and Nikolayev (right). In another version of the same photo, the mystery cosmonaut's face is smudged beyond recognition; in the final version, the background is completely blacked out.

that despite all the data gathered, there was no proof that any Russian spacemen had been accidentally killed. As a matter of fact, a convincing circumstantial argument could be made that no Russians had secretly died in space at all. Since then, of course, two different Soviet space teams have been wiped out on widely broadcast space missions. Their deaths were quickly revealed to the world, and the men were given heroic public funerals in Moscow (in 1967 and in 1971).

What I discovered was much more substantial. Beginning in 1960, the U.S.S.R. had been regularly retouching its cosmonaut group photographs to conceal the existence of certain space trainees. First I found one "before" and "after" set, then another. In reviewing old Soviet space newsreels, I found a whole secret cast of space characters who have never publicly appeared in Russia. The Moscow censors have been doing their best to conceal the existence of these men from the world.

What happened to them? They were obviously training for future missions, and their colleagues who went to flight school with them did indeed fly into space to glory and fame. Yet we do

Who is this mysterious missing cosmonaut (Anatoliy? Grigori? Some other name?)? Who . . . .

not even know the names of these others.

As it turned out, Khrushchev was pounding his shoe at the U.N. because some rockets aimed at Mars had blown up; there were no men involved. At the same time, a rocket had exploded unexpectedly on the launch pad, killing dozens of top space officials. (Khrushchev admits this in his posthumously published memoirs.) Those radio reports from Europe were either mistakes or outright fantasy, as later even more farfetched claims by the

... prepares for a centrifuge run in a 1962 film;

same "radio eavesdroppers" soon demonstrated. Other rumors of "secret dead Russian spacemen" were as easily dispelled.

But where does that leave our real mystery missing space pilots? What did they do—or have done to them—to deserve the enforced anonymity of the cutting room floor? Why the forger's airbrush for so many young, smiling, confident trainees? What fatal, or shameful, or crippling events relegated these spacemen to dark oblivion while their luckier colleagues literally soared toward the stars and returned to worldwide fame and acclaim?

The existence of these men was completely unsuspected until 1971, when the Soviets published a new book on their space program, a glowing, hero-worshipping, tedious propaganda work designed to offset some of the bad publicity resulting from the recent deaths of the Soyuz XI trio. The author was a Soviet journalist named Yevgeniy Riabchikov, chief space correspondent. In Russia, the job of space correspondents is not so much to report on space events as to use these events to glorify communism. Those events which do not fit are either altered or omitted.

... stands at right on a volleyball court;

Skimming briefly over the turgid and colorless prose, I turned to a section of photographs with the enticing label, "Published for the first time." Soviet censors, like any overgrown government bureaucracy, have too much paperwork and have too many things to keep secret, so they often make mistakes and let things slip through; that hope keeps researchers like myself motivated.

I was not disappointed. In the U.S. edition of this 1971 book were a series of photographs taken ten years before at Sochi. This resort town on the Black Sea was the scene of a month-long vacation for the Soviet team responsible for the successful flight of the world's first man in space, Red Air Force Major Yuri

... attends a reception for the airforce Chief of Staff (he sits between Popovich, left, and Khrunov, right);

Gagarin. Several group photographs showed men I did not recognize, space personalities who had never before been seen in the West.

About the same time, I received a set of old Russian space propaganda films made between 1961 and 1963. They had been given to an American writer while he was researching a book in Moscow, and he had passed them on to the Cape Canaveral historical archives when he was finished with them. I was the first person to view these films in a decade, and when I saw what was in them I patiently went through them frame by frame at a photo studio. The same mystery men appeared, and there were no doubts now: here were several (I know of at least eight) spacemen who later disappeared.

There was still nothing very sinister about all this. In the American space program, numerous trainees have dropped out of the program without making a space flight. Several have been grounded for medical reasons. A few who were trained almost fifteen years ago are still waiting for a flight. And a handful have been killed in training accidents or ordinary aircraft crashes. The same might have happened to these Russians and it did not appear to be anything unusual. I filed a report with my colleagues and turned my attention elsewhere.

But the big surprise was out there, waiting for me. The following year I received several new books from Moscow on their space efforts. I can read Russian, but their publications about space usually bore me to tears because of the incessant

... lurks in the background in a group photo (Leonov, at left);

unimaginative, repetitive, and overwhelming propaganda slant. As usual, I turned to the photograph section first.

One group picture looked familiar, but with a difference. I rushed to my bookshelf and pulled down the Riabchikov volume. Leafing through it, I found the photograph as I had remembered it. However, a man had now been erased from the back row, and he had been one of my "mystery men." Now he was a "mystery *missing* man." Where he had been standing, a new rose bush now bloomed and dark shadows loomed.

The forgery immediately raised a compelling question: Why had this been done? What motivation had been behind this obvious effort to conceal the existence of this man from the world? And how had the omnipotent Russian censors slipped up by releasing the unaltered photo as well?

The last question seemed to be the easiest. Riabchikov was the chief space correspondent and apparently had used his authority and his private photo archives to illustrate the American edition of his book, realizing full well that few people would be interested in it without such added features. (He was completely correct. Originally sold at $9.95, the book was within a year being "remaindered" in bargain book basements in New York for $1.00, and few people were willing to pay even that much for it!) So he chose the "New" photos, more than ten years old, and bypassed the bureaucratic chain to do so. The European editions, released a few months later, did not include this set of photographs.

It's ironic: For many years, skeptical Western observers have suspected that Moscow has been forging space photographs in an attempt to prove that Russia had carried out some spectacular space feat, when in reality it was all a hoax. Now I had several real sets of forged Russian space photos. Did they prove that Russia had carried out some feat that it did not want the world to find out about? Had these men suffered some fate which Moscow was determined to keep hidden? It was a puzzle designed to warm the heart of any researcher.

Examining the old movies, I had found so many unknown space trainees that I was forced to resort to codes to identify and keep track of them all. I had labeled them, in arbitrary order, "X-1," "X-2," "X-3," and so forth. The erased man had been my X-2. Later, I was to discover that X-1 was the chief Soviet space trainer, which explained why he dressed like the trainees and was so often photographed with them. But my "X" family has been growing larger every year, and so has the collection of "before" and "after" forged photographs.

Alerted now as to what to look for, I returned to earlier photographs and sought evidence of tampering with originals. Many Soviet space pictures looked funny due to poor photo and printing techniques, and a good number were obviously retouched, generally to hide background details while leaving the smiling faces of the spacemen suspended, as it were, in space.

It didn't take long to find additional cases. A photograph of the crew bus on the way to the launch of Voskhod 2 in 1965 shows a man peering over the shoulder of cosmonaut Aleksey Leonov (the same Russian pilot who took part in the 1975 space linkup with our Apollo capsule). But another photo shows only an open

...sits at the far right when Gagarin (standing, center) is designated as prime pilot for Vostok 1;

window: somebody's head had obviously been lopped off in the photograph! What happened in real life?

The man "X-2" showed up again. He was the escort for Gagarin on the bus to the launch pad in 1961. One photo released in a foreign language pamphlet clearly shows him standing behind the seated, space suited Gagarin. I had previously known he had been there because he was plainly visible in a movie sequence released in 1967. But like the Cheshire cat in *Alice in Wonderland*, he was doomed to slowly fade away, leaving not even his smile behind. Another photograph shows his body all right, but his face is just a blur, a clumsy thumbprint smear designed to hide his identity but not his existence. That trick was left to the next edition, where the previous sloppy work was touched up. Now there was no background at all, just a blank gray tone behind the shoulders of the world's first man in space; "X-2" was gone completely.

But he has left some traces beyond the images on a few surviving frames of film. After some more work, I thought I even knew his first name.

During the early years of the space age, Soviet journalists including Riabchikov often visited the space training center outside Moscow. They reported on activity and painted glorious

... escorts Gagarin to the launch pad (and feeds him a "good luck caramel," according to Gagarin's memoirs);

character sketches for Soviet youth to emulate (the characterization in Soviet space books is understandably two-dimensional and cardboard: the writers are describing propaganda posters, not real human beings). These space heroes could not be identified completely, lest one of them disgrace himself by failing some crucial test and, not being a fit model for young communists, be dropped from the program. So in the written dispatches, only the first names of the men were used.

By and large, we later found out who these men were. "Valery" was Valery Bykovsky, who flew in Vostok V in 1963. "Pavel" (Belyayev) flew on Voskhod II, and "Georgi" and "Viktor" flew on Soyuz flights in 1969. But three other names were mentioned by the journalists, names that have never appeared on the front pages of *Pravda*. Three men had either changed their names or vanished from the program, they were Grigori, Ivan, and Valentin: or so I thought.

"Grigori" was, by the 1960-62 newspaper accounts, a very important trainee, classed with Gagarin, Popovich, and others in the top of his group. In the Riabchikov photos and the early movies, one of the "X" pilots obviously fills this description. It is

... monitors the progress of the Vostok-3 & 4 mission in 1962, with comrades Komarov (left) and Bykovsky (center); and who then vanishes from the pages (and photographs) of Soviet Space History.

"X-2," the erased man in the Sochi photographs.

Grigori "X-2" was one of the six men picked for the Vostok program, and was one of the four finalists for the very first manned space flight on April 12, 1961. The other three men flew the first, second, and third Vostok missions during the following year. Grigori vanished.

When I first published these pictures in the British magazine *Spaceflight* in 1973-74, I was unable to answer the most fundamental question: Why? Where was Grigori and his missing comrades? Were they, fallen from favor for some indiscretion or misjudgment, assigned to a remote Siberian jet interceptor squadron? Were they in prison or labor camp for some real or imaginary political offense (as suggested by historian Robert Conquest in 1975 in the newsletter *Soviet Analyst*)? Did they lie in distant, anonymous graves? Or were their ashes mixed with the wreckage of their demolished spaceship deep on the floor of some ocean?

In an attempt to smoke out the answer, I distributed copies of their photographs far and wide for publication. American astronauts brought the pictures to Russia during training sessions for the Apollo Soyuz mission in 1974-1975; their

Two 'classic' examples of recent communist photographic forgeries:
First, Czech revisionist leader Alexander Dubcek is removed from an official
government portrait released after the Soviet Army overthrew the Czech government in 1968;

cosmonaut colleagues only smiled and changed the subject, but
one high Soviet cosmonaut *did* confess that "six or eight"
cosmonaut trainees *had died* in training before their first space
missions (the comparable U.S. figure is eight). American
newsmen, armed with the photos and smelling a good story,
badgered the cosmonauts during interviews and news
conferences, but were rewarded only with vague comments about
unspecified "medical disqualifications."

Second, Mao tse-Tung's wife, shown during the difficult "Long March" in 1930's, did not survive the history books written after Mao's death, when she was purged as part of the "Gang of Four" conspiracy—

Obviously reacting to the growing embarrassment of a widely-known clumsy space coverup, the Moscow propaganda machine creaked and groaned—and spat out an answer. It may not be *the* answer (I've still got my suspicions.) but it was a remarkable response to bring "goosed" by a western private researcher.

The form it took was that of a set of memoirs by cosmonaut Georgi Shonin, one of the first group of cosmonauts. The book (The Very First, 1977) concentrated mainly on detailing how Shonin was a perfect patriot and communist, but several pages revealed hitherto-unadmitted information. According to Shonin, there actually had been twenty men in the first cosmonaut class, of whom only twelve were to fly: Shonin admitted that eight of the men had been dropped for medical or academic reasons! Their first names were Valentin, Anatoliy, Valentin Junior, Grigori, Ivan, Valentin "Grampa," Mars (a Tartar), and Dmitriy. So there *had* been an Ivan and a Grigori, but there were *three* Valentins!

Several of the men were dropped for medical reasons, including Valentin # 1 (the most promising pilot in the group), Anatoliy (who couldn't tolerate centrifuge overloads), Valentin "Grampa" (who was just too old), and Dmitriy (who trained for nine years before being eliminated in 1969). The other four were expelled for what Shonin delicately styled "an inability to conform to strict cosmonaut discipline and academic standards." But oddly, despite the earlier private confession that many cosmonauts had *died* in training, none of these non-official eight cosmonaut drop-outs had allegedly been among them. That just does not ring true, so perhaps, Shonin's book has not been *entirely* candid either—although it's gone a long way. (I still want to know their *last* names, too.)

These young men, and the nameless others who did die in training accidents, deserve better from history. Apollo astronauts left on the moon a small statue (representing a fallen astronaut) and a memorial plaque containing a list of all the men who have died in space or in preparation for space flights. It includes the names of Americans who never made it into space, fallen would-be spacemen who in Russia would be relegated to the status of "non-persons." This moon plaque (which was emplaced in 1971, and mercifully, has *not* required a *single* known addition since then) is clearly incomplete without the Russian names. Continued Western pressure may compel more Soviet candor which may, some day, reveal those names and true fates: that is the least of the debts the future owes them.

CHAPTER NINE
The "Jellyfish UFO" Dilemma

A uniquely valuable "control run" UFO encounter occurred over northwestern Russia before dawn on September 20, 1977. Residents of the city of Petrozavodsk were terrified to observe a giant glowing "jellyfish UFO" hovering over them; subsequent accounts chronicled physical, psychological, and electromagnetic effects, as well as radar confirmation. The strange light was also seen in the skies over Leningrad and Helsinki.

This frightening apparition was, in fact, the launching of the Kosmos-955 spy satellite from the secret Soviet "Northern Cosmodrome" near Plesetsk. The base, which began operation in 1966 and now accounts for more than half of the world's satellite launchings, has never been officially acknowledged by Moscow; it only came to the attention of the public at all through the keen observations and computations of Geoffrey Perry's "Kettering Group" of schoolboy space observers in England.

The identification of the "jellyfish UFO" (as it came to be called in the Western press) with Kosmos-955's booster contrails took only a few hours, and was subsequently publicized widely. However, these published reports were evidently not circulated inside the USSR, where the encounter had excited tremendous popular interest. Through the embellishments of Soviet amateur UFO buffs, the "jellyfish UFO" story quietly germinated and then burst forth renewed in the spring of 1978 in the *National Enquirer*. By the following year, it was firmly enshrined in the popular UFO pantheon. (Despite its rejection by responsible UFO proponents.)

For the Soviet government, meanwhile, the case has become an acute embarrassment. However hostile the official propaganda apparatus may be to UFOs, an authentic explanation of the "Petrozavodsk phenomenon" (as it was neutrally known in official Soviet circles) was unthinkable, since the Plesetsk rocket center was a military secret. Consequently, it became necessary for Soviet scientists (who are probably well aware of the activities of the Northern Cosmodrome) to issue a series of lame "explanations" that have been quite ineffective. This current impasse seems inescapable as the popularity of this UFO story continues to spread inside and outside Russia; it could well be the most electrifying UFO story ever whispered about inside the USSR.

The earliest published account of the Petrozavodsk phenomenon was written by local Tass correspondent Nikolay Milov: "On September 20 at about 0400 a huge star suddenly flared up in the dark sky, impulsively sending shafts of light to the earth," wrote the correspondent in a story headlined "Unusual Natural Phenomenon Observed in Karelia." Milov continued: "This star moved slowly towards Petrozavodsk and, spreading out over it in the form of a jellyfish, hung there, showering the city with a multitude of very fine rays which created an image of pouring rain. After some time the luminescent rays ceased. The jellyfish turned into a bright semicircle and resumed its movement in the direction of Lake Onega. ... A semicircular pool of bright light, red in the middle and white at the sides, then formed in this shroud. This phenomenon lasted ten to twelve minutes."

When this report reached Moscow two days later (by mail?), the Tass international wire editor evidently did not associate it with anything in his thick book of "don't tells"—so the story went out that afternoon over both domestic and foreign news lines. Western correspondents quickly dubbed it a UFO and it was reported as such in a United Press International story from Moscow (in which reports from Helsinki were also quoted describing a light seen in the sky for four minutes over the Finnish capital).

My own involvement with the case began on September 23, 1977, when the story was carried in American newspapers under such headlines as "UFO Sighted Over Northwest Russia: Similar Object Observed in Finland." But based on my personal observations of nighttime rocket shots and on my familiarity

The city of Petrozavodsk was terrified by a pre-dawn "UFO Attack" in 1977 which has become the most sensational UFO story to ever come out of Russia. Photograph courtesy of Novosti; taken by V. Syomin

with Soviet space flight operations, I immediately suspected a Plesetsk launching. A quick telephone call to the satellite tracking information center at NASA's Goddard Space Flight Center (just outside of Washington, D.C.) confirmed that a satellite had been lofted into a particularly high orbit from Plesetsk on the morning of September 20th; computations based on detailed tracking data supplied to NASA by the North American Air Defense Command showed that the launch had been at approximately 3:58 a.m. local time.

Such predawn high angle launchings are in fact quite infrequent of Plesetsk. Searching over thirteen years of records, I found listing for only three earlier cases: Kosmos-184 on October 24, 1967; Meteor-2 on October 6, 1969; and Meteor-9 on July 16, 1971. The second of these cases was written up by observers in Finland, who told the British Interplanetary Society that "there rose a small bright object from the east. It slowly arched upward, culminated in the northeast at a height of about twenty-five degrees and started descending. . . . The object drew three misty arcs of light on the sky. The brightest of these was right behind it and the two others on both sides. The object was brighter than the narrow crescent Moon, and cast faint shadows on the ground. In three minutes there was a phenomenon like a gas cloud; the object was shrouded by some obscuring matter, and was seen through it

163

much dimmed....According to Finnish newspapers, the phenomenon was observed from many places all over the country, and at least from two aircraft....The phenomenon stayed over the horizon of my observing position for at least four minutes."

Such launchings from Plesetsk are usually *not* seen from northwest Russia because of pervasive pre-dawn cloud cover. But one witness to the "jellyfish UFO" made a valuable observation when he testified that "the weather was highly unusual—crisp and clear."

This and similar reports prompted Dr. Charles Sheldon, the U.S. Library of Congress expert on the USSR space program, to write in *Soviet Space Exploration* (1975) that "when weather conditions are just right, an occasional Plesetsk launch has been visible from Sweden and Finland, when the still firing rocket rises above the horizon." And that's what happened in this case. Another official Moscow news bulletin released routinely the day before news of the UFO came out, gave these dry facts:

> Launching of Kosmos-955—An artificial earth satellite, Kosmos-955, was launched September 20, 1977 from the Soviet Union. The satellite is carrying scientific apparatus for the continuation of space exploration. The satellite was launched into orbit with the parameters: initial period of revolution—97.5 minutes; apogee.—664 kilometers; perigee—631 kilometers; orbit inclination—81.2 degrees.
> The satellite's onboard apparatus is functioning normally.

But Western space observers have long since learned to penetrate through the web of deception and misinformation which Moscow weaves around its space effort. They were able to determine that Kosmos-955 was NOT launched from Russia's public space center, the Baikonur Cosmodrome (called Tyuratam by the West), but was launched *from Plesetsk*. Furthermore, the satellite was not a 'scientific' payload participating in 'space exploration.' Moscow was lying: the satellite was a space spy, designed to eavesdrop on Western microwave communications and radar signatures.

Within a few days (September 27th), a UFO research group in the U.S. issued a press release identifying the "jellyfish UFO" event with the Kosmos-955 launch. Investigators at the Center for UFO Studies in Evanston, Ill., had formed similar suspicions about the nature of the "UFO" and were happy to receive confirmation from my own calculations; on September 30th, a United Press International story from Chicago reported the essence of this explanation and attributed it to me, "a researcher for the UFO center." The center's own publication, *The*

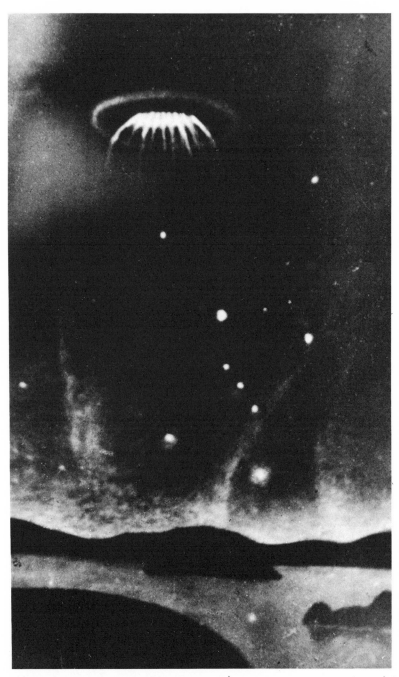

Artwork from inside Russia shows the UFO and its tentacles above the constellation Orion. Courtesy of Coleman Von Keviczky

International UFO Reporter, published the results in its October 1977 issue; other more widely circulated magazines did likewise. Despite the fact that the story rapidly dropped out of the international UFO literature almost as soon as it had sprung up, it was receiving a far different reception inside Russia. There, ardent UFO amateurs began collecting eyewitness accounts and secondhand and thirdhand stories of what had really happened that morning in Petrozavodsk. When two American newsmen traveling in Moscow called on a few of their contacts in the Russian UFO movement the following March, they were presented with an incredible story of what came to be headlined as "The First UFO to Inflict Damage on a City."

As described by William Dick and Henry Gris in the *National Enquirer* (April 18, 1978), the UFO's rays had drilled holes in paving stones and through windows—and all of this evidence had been collected by the KGB, so there weren't any samples to actually see. A group of longshoremen thought it was an American nuclear attack and screamed: "This is the end!" A doctor reported that his ambulance went out of control when the UFO appeared. The air reportedly smelled of ozone.

All of Russia's leading "UFO experts" endorsed the UFO nature of the encounter, according to Dick and Gris. Aleksandr Kazantsev, famous for his "ancient astronaut" evidence, announced that "As far as I am concerned it was a spaceship from outer space, carrying out reconnaissance." Vladimir Azhazha, who was recently quoted widely as claiming that Apollo 11 was shadowed by UFOs on the moon, asserted: "In my opinion what was seen over Petrozavodsk was either a UFO, a carrier of high intelligence, with crew and passengers, or it was a field of energy created by such a UFO." Aleksey Zolotov, champion of the theory of extraterrestrial origin of the 1908 Tunguska blast, told Dick and Gris: "In my opinion, the object was a typical flying saucer. The available reports left no doubt whatsoever in mind, clearly indicating the UFO nature of the event. I, myself, know it was a UFO." Lastly, Felix Zigel, astronomy lecturer and dean of Russian UFOlogists, also agreed that the object was a "true UFO." "Without a doubt," he told the *National Enquirer*, "It had all the features."

The official Soviet reaction to this groundswell of popular interest (bordering on hysteria at times) was to trot out a series of scientists to assure the public that all was well. Vladimir Krat, director of the Pulkovo Observatory, had told reporters on September 23rd that "at present it is still difficult to explain its origin with complete certainty," but by October 12th he was telling the world that "the phenomenon was probably a rocket stage burning up. The visibility depends on the materials of the sputnik. Sputniks can explode on reentry sometimes and the products of the explosion can remain in the air for a long time."

When it became clear that this was not convincing anyone, a new explanation was cranked out. In mid-August, 1978, an "M. Dmitriyev, Doctor of Chemical Sciences," published a report in *Aviation and Cosmonautics* monthly to the effect that the cloud was a "chemoluminescence zone" enhanced by nitrous oxide pollution from the factories in Petrozavodsk.

In what I have dubbed the "swampsky gas" gambit (named in honor of the Air Force explanation for some 1966 Michigan UFOs), Dmitriyev presented his explanation (this, excerpted from a Library of Congress translation and summary):

The phenomenon was due to the formation of an airglow zone in the atmosphere, a so-called ChL (chemiluminescence) zone. A rather detailed definition of chemiluminescent zones is given. The article discusses any possible effects of ChL zones on the mind of pilots and on the functioning of onboard control systems and instruments. After all observation data from Petrozavodsk were processed, it was determined that the intensity of the flare's optical radiation in the ChL zone reached 15 cal/cm^2/min; the concentration of chemiluminescent matter was 50 mg/m^3 for ozone and 25 mg/m^3 for nitrogen oxide. Pollution contributes greatly to the intensity of such flares. Hence, any danger of ChL zones for the operation of aircraft depends on the concentration and size. Chemiluminescent emmission per se is harmless, in both the optical and infrared ranges. However, the ChL zones may act as sources of radioemission which affects the functioning of electronic devices, especially causing disturbances in radar equipment operation. Further, all chemiluminescent matters are toxic if present in high concentrations: they may penetrate an aircraft cabin and adversely affect the crew. Color is a good indicator of the ChL zone toxicity: dark or light-blue indicates the prevalence of ozone and oxygen atoms; these are more toxic than nitrogen oxide or dioxide, colored red or orange. Even a low-intensity ChL zone may have a narcotic effect on the crew, as demonstrated by the crews of six U.S. "Avengers" on a bright sunny day over the Atlantic Ocean (Bermuda Triangle). Often when an aircraft enters the ChL zone, a sharp irritating smell is recorded inside the cabin. At a very high concentration of energy in the Chl zone, the zone not only gleams but is capable of producing explosions similar to ball lightning. The size of the explosive zone is relatively small, some 1-1.5 meters, but such a zone should nevertheless be avoided by aircraft or rockets, i.e., pilots should be guided by visual and radar observations and try to bypass them. The crew should always be "mentally" aware of the existence of such zones; they should understand the possible changes in the color of skies, the appearance of an intense gleam, and the unusual sharp smell. They should also double their attention, since the ChL zone not only affects the mind, but also the functioning of electronic and radar equipment.

Perhaps Dmitreyev himself had strayed too close to such a zone. His mental gymnastics and scientific razzle-dazzle are enough to numb the mind of any reader, and perhaps that was his real purpose!

Evidently hoping to gain in quantity what was lacking in quality, Soviet press officials issued yet another "explanation" in January, 1979, when Dr. V. V. Migulin, recently tagged as the Academy of Science's UFO contact man, attributed the phenomenon to "physical changes in the upper atmosphere," probably geomagnetic in origin. Writing in *La Recherche* (Paris, July-August 1979), Migulin further explained how a shower of solar electrons had been channeled into the upper atmosphere at this particular point by a magnetic storm.

Migulin, in a private communication to me, ruled out the satellite launching explanation because the object had been seen over a wide area and over a period of four hours. Gris had also made a similar objection during telephone conversations; the reports that he had received indicated that the object had circled Petrozavodsk and had visited other cities at significantly different times.

Such discrepancies cannot shake the ironclad identification of the original phenomenon with the rocket launching, since the times and the details of the best descriptions tally too exactly with the launching for coincidence. The embellishments of these reports, however, can be useful in understanding and gauging the reliability of similar reports of other UFO encounters for which the original stimulus is not initially known. This experience confirms the astute observations of astronomer Frank Drake, whose paper "On the Abilities and Limitations of Witnesses" appeared in *UFOs-Scientific Debate* (1972). Wrote Drake:

A witness's memory of such exotic events...fades very quickly. After one day, about half of the reports are clearly

Dusk Launch of Soyuz-13 (1973) showed "tentacles" which still converged because of low altitude. Courtesy of the Author's collection

erroneous; after two days, about three-quarters are clearly erroneous; after four days, only ten percent are good; after five days, people report more imagination than truth. It became clear that later they were reconstructing in their imagination an event based on some dim memory of what happened. This is something that the UFO investigator rarely appreciates.

According to Drake, this garble factor will destroy the effectiveness of reports of an object's motion, position, and speed unless investigators collect the accounts very quickly. This evidently did happen at Petrozavodsk, and the story grew over the passing months, eventually including some purely mythical elements such as the holes that nobody actually saw, and some coincidental elements such as a far-from-unusual failure of a municipal computer system on the morning of the event.

Witness testimony is not the only source of garble in UFO stories; the following is the highly inaccurate account of the Petrozavodsk UFO as written up by German UFO "expert" Johannes von Buttiar:

> On 20 September 1977 at around four o'clock in the afternoon [sic!], a gigantic disc [sic!] appeared over the Soviet town of Petrozavodsk on the western shore of Lake Onega. It was 'as big as a football field' [sic!], in the words of the inhabitants....The UFO had directed five intense beams of light [sic!] onto the town. Holes were found burned into windowpanes and paving stones....The internationally known Soviet geophysicist Alexei Zolotov [sic!] commented: 'In my opinion it was a typical UFO.' "

The respected British periodical *Flying Saucer Review* (widely considered the best UFO journal in the world) printed all the initial wild reports without ever later publishing clarifications or retractions. And Gordon Creighton of FSR endorsed the case again in 1981 as a true UFO event. Meanwhile, *UFO Report*, the most serious-minded of the American pulp UFO magazines, told its readers that the damage to the city was caused by the explosion of the space rocket.

Other crackpot groups have adopted the "Jellyfish UFO" as their own. In Canada, a group called the "Planetary Association for Clean Energy" (devoted to a mystic vision of the magic of Nikola Tesla) denounced the *National Enquirer* UFO story as "a story concocted by high level Soviet intelligence sources."

The purpose, according to group spokesman Hugh F. Cochrane, was:

> ...covering up a dangerous blunder caused by experi-

Another view of "tentacles" associated with Semyorka booster launches. Courtesy of the Author's collection

ments being conducted by their own intercontinental ballistic missile defense command. Based on this new evidence it now appears that the 'UFO attack' was in reality a malfunction of a high energy beam weapon which almost brought disaster to the Russian city....Their high energy beam encountered particle obstructions in the atmosphere. These send the beam on a wild excursion. Thus, the brilliant glow in the sky was not a galactic vehicle, but a glowing plasmic shell. And the 'ray beams' were laser-like splatters of the beam deflected downward where the energy was absorbed, boring holes in glass windows and paving blocks.

An added dimension to the "Jellyfish UFO" can be afforded by more eyewitness accounts recently received from Finland and Estonia. The following material has been especially translated for this report and has never before appeared in English. Together with Russian reports of physical damage in Petrozavodsk, these accounts transform the "Jellyfish UFO" into a classic "Radar-Visual" *and* "Close Encounter of the *Second* kind."

The Finnish newspaper "Kansan Uutiset" reported the day

after the sighting that "Those who were up early indeed rubbed their eyes when a fast moving bright phenomenon of light flew past the capital, Helsinki, at 3:06 AM (4:06 AM Moscow time), and continued its voyage toward the north." Dr. Matti Kivinen of the Nurmijaren Geophysical Observatory suggested it was a re-entering spacecraft. The "Kansan Uutiset" article subsequently was mentioned in the Moscow newspaper *Trud*, which told Russian readers that the object had been visible in Helsinki for four minutes and that Helsinki airport radar had tracked the object moving toward the east.

Sightings of the UFO were also reported from Estonia, at Poltsama, Turi, Luva, Ihamarusta, Taikse, and Kanep. Rays of light pointing to the Earth were seen. Elmar Jorgen, living in Poltsama (forty miles north of Dorpat-Tartu), saw the object at 4:08 AM. According to him, it was a source of light about the size of a human head, sending off rays of light. It flew very slowy about twenty degrees above the horizon, from southwest to north. The source of light was inside a fog, and on the top of the object dark stripes could be seen. Dairymaid Linda Hermann, fifty-seven, from Luva in the Polva district twenty miles south of Dorpat, saw an extremely bright "star" a few minutes after 4:00 AM. It rose slowly higher, and then sent out a ray of light. Hermann reported that the single ray disappeared as the object reached an elevation of twenty to twenty-five degrees, after which six rays of light and a corolla-like circle formed. The UFO moved to the north at a high rate of speed, sending off two more rays of light *upwards* as it illuminated the sky with a circulating dim rainbow above the rays. The UFO was in sight for about five minutes.

An intriguing account (published by M. Toivola, a local UFO expert, in the magazine *Ultra*) came from Turku, Finland, on the coast of the Baltic. Two men were on their way to a garbage dump outside of town at about 3:10 AM (4:10 AM Petrozavodsk time). They saw a strange light phenomenon which they estimated to be about a quarter of a mile away across a field, at the edge of some woods. The gaseous, incandescent rotating smoke ring seemed about thirty feet in diameter and was surrounded by a fog although the edges of the circle were distinct. As the UFO ascended it grew larger—until suddenly the fiery ring disappeared and the object changed into a uniform ball which seemed to approach the two frightened witnesses. They ran back to the car as the object rose higher in the sky, expanding and growing dimmer. As they drove off they saw the UFO behind them—almost a classic "car-chasing UFO."

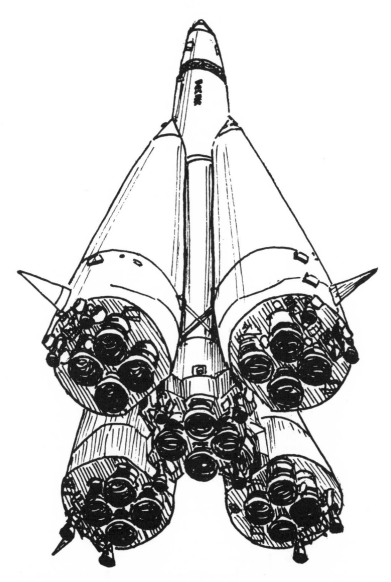

Business End of Semyorka (ss-6, or "A-class") booster shows multiple engines and strap-on sections which result in startling "Jellyfish tentacles" appearance of contrails. Courtesy of the Library of Congress

Yuri Gromov, director of the meteorological observatory in the city, was on duty when the UFO appeared. He described the shafts-of-light phenomenon. Then: "Suddenly a smaller body detached itself and veered off. Meanwhile the main body gradually took the shape of an elliptic ring, pinkish red in the middle, with white rim. It moved toward the cloud cover over Lake Onega, burned a red hole in it, and gradually vanished.... There were no aircraft—planes or helicopters—flying in the area at that time and the weather was good. The sky was clear and the object definitely was not ball lightning."

Tass correspondent Milov interviewed at least a hundred eyewitnesses, and used that data to fix the diameter of the UFO at about 350 feet. The number is based on reports that the craft came in low over the harbor and hovered over a ship which was later found to be 465 feet long. Many witnesses reacted wildly, Milov noted, "as though they had been taken ill and had become mentally confused. There was no doubt in my mind as I interrogated them that I was facing people who had come face to face with an incredible event."

Throughout 1979-80, new information and evaluations of the "Petrozavodsk phenomenon" continued to appear. "Exciting new information has been seeping through from Petrozavodsk concerning a spaceship that visited the area recently," announced Russian UFO buff Aleksandr Kazantsev. The latest description of the "Jellyfish" is that "it hung in the night sky for at least two hours at an altitude of sixty miles." In the words of a local journalist, "It was the center of great activity as much smaller bodies appeared to dart away from it, while others seemed to approach and disappear into immense portholes." Moscow physicist Vladimir Azhazha again endorsed the UFO character of the event: "In my view, it was a mother ship from outer space. Its appearance seems to indicate that an extraterrestrial civilization is in the final stage prior to direct communication with the Earth."

Professor Migulin remains publicly positive that it was "a rare and impressive natural phenomenon," although he continues to solicit UFO reports (his address: Department of General Physics and Astronomy, USSR Academy of Sciences, 117071-Moscow, Leninsky Prospekt #14). In his latest report, November 1979, he described his reconstruction of the whole encounter:

This rare and impressive natural phenomenon was observed over the entire north-western region of the Soviet Union at about 4:00 on September 20, 1977. The active process, on the whole, developed for about three hours. At the culminating moment a very bright glowing phenomenon with a reddish nucleus, a radiant or jet envelope and a subsequent prolonged and stable amorphous glow was observed in the Petrozavodsk area (Karelia). At the moment of the maximum development of the envelopes the nucleus retained a fixed position for five to ten minutes. There are even reports about a bright ray which emanated for a short period from the center and about the division of the nucleus. Most observers agree that after the jet process came to an end the glowing nucleus began to move in approximately the opposite direction and hid itself in the clouds. This picture was observed in several populated centers and aroused great interest among the public. This has led to a number of hasty, amateur and superficial studies of the phenomenon, all of which are far from scientific. They have resulted in various hypotheses about the nature of the phenomenon. However, none of them in my opinion, correspond to the truth and range from a globe lightning, the fall or the launching of an artificial earth satellite and chemiluminescence to the visit of the persons from another planet to the Earth.

The official Soviet UFO-explainer confidently concluded:

The first serious studies have shown that the moment when the Petrozavodsk phenomenon was observed was quite unique from the point of view of solar activity and the condition of the atmosphere and the magnetosphere. At that moment, a noise storm and a flux of solar electrons simultaneously reached the Earth; the magnetosphere proved to be in a very excited state, and in the lower atmosphere over the north-west of the Soviet Union the front of a giant cyclone with small cyclones was passing by. Showers alternated with clear weather within half an hour. At an altitude of about 36,000 feet a powerful jet of an air flow moved at speeds of up to 300 miles per hour. In the north, intensive aurorae of rare types were observed and to the south thunderstorms occurred.

After cataloguing all these coincidences, Migulin declared that:

It would have been most surprising if on this night nothing had been observed over Karelia....If, as a result of studies, we succeed in determining the physical factors which caused this phenomenon, then it will become possible to simulate this phenomenon and to investigate it experimentally, which would be a major step towards the understanding of the UFO problem. It can be stated in conclusion that the basic immediate task is to avoid sensationalism, to make a serious and careful analysis of the essence of the processes which cause the UFO phenomena. Statistical, theoretical and experimental investigations and the participation of specialists in various branches of science in the solution of this problem will be of help.

Migulin's need for experimental repetitions of the "Petrozavodsk UFO," and the desires of Moscow UFO buffs for more flying saucer evidence, might well be satisfied by an article in the March 1979 issue of *Tahdet Ja Avaruus* (Finnish for "space and astronomy"). Two charts and several photographs were included in an article about Plesetsk rocket launchings observed from Finland. Although few were as spectacular as the September 20, 1977 event (which was on the list), they all represented a phenomenon with which Finnish astronomers had grown quite familiar (my thanks to the source of this material, a leading Finnish astronomer who did not wish his name publicly attached to the subject of UFOs).

The lists included "Meteor" weather satellites, "Molniya" communications satellites, several "Kosmos" spy satellites, plus many rocket launchings which were never acknowledged in Moscow. This list has an average of two entries per year although some years had more (such as 1977, with five, including the Petrozavodsk "Jellyfish"), so more than just the high-altitude launches I referred to earlier were actually visible. So the Finns have already conducted Professor Migulin's "UFO experiments," and since they are not bound by the security gags which compel Migulin to try to distract public attention from the *real* cause of the Petrozavodsk UFO, they have published the results—except that nobody outside of Finland, least of all the UFO enthusiasts in Moscow has noticed!

It is ironic that one feature of super-secret Plesetsk has been trumpeted by Moscow. True, no mention had ever been made of the missile center. All Soviet space launchings, according to the official falsehoods, come from the Baikonur Cosmodrome (even that name is a falsehood—the site is hundreds of miles from Baikonur, much nearer to the small town of Tyuratam) or occasionally from a small site near the Volga River called Kapustin Yar.

But Moscow will not let America forget about this scenario from true history of Plesetsk:

Under the command of Lieutenant John Baker, the two platoons of Company K, 339th infantry regiment, crossed the small river upstream of their goal under cover of winter darkness. The enemy was caught by surprise at dawn, and the American assault carried the town. But hostile artillery on hills above the road leading southwest blocked the advance of the American

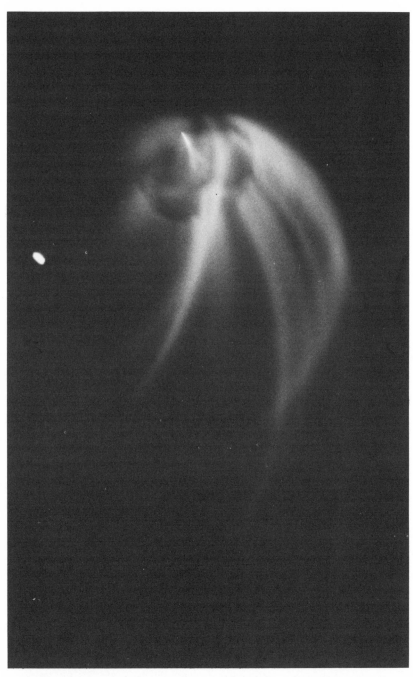

Actual photograph of the contrails of Kosmos-955, viewed from Finland.
Courtesy of Jukka Mikkola.

soldiers towards their goal, a rail center forty miles away that was the main staging point for enemy action on this front.

The Americans dug in. Eventually, under pounding from the entrenched artillery on the slopes above the small abandoned village, the two platoons withdrew back across the river.

What Moscow does not forget or forgive is that this scene did not take place in France or in Italy or in Haiti or on Guadalcanal or in Korea: it took place in north Russia.

The year was 1919. The river was the Emta, and the small town was called Kodish. The enemy was the Red Army of Russia. The railhead objective, which the Americans and their unreliable "White Russian" allies were never to reach, was called PLESETSK.

For almost half a century, the town of Plesetsk continued to slumber in the obscurity it well deserved—and which Moscow news censors now try frantically to perpetuate. But nine years after the first Sputnik was launched from Baikonur, Plesetsk became the scene for new artillery fire in the Soviet-American conflict. The thunder of mighty rockets was heard. Satellites climbed into space from newly constructed launch pads.

Although Western intelligence agencies obviously knew a great deal about Plesetsk as a space base, they could not reveal their information to the public. The revelation of the existence of a new Russian space base came instead from an English school master and his adolescent radio amateurs.

Under the direction of Geoffrey Perry, a science teacher at the Kettering Grammar School in northeastern Britain, students had set up a space listening post as a class project. By using surplus military and amateur radio equipment, this small dedicated group was able to eavesdrop on the space telemetry signals broadcast by Soviet satellites. Knowing the duration, strength, and type of the signals, the students were able to plot the paths of the satellites and make good guesses about their purposes.

Early in 1966, Moscow announced the launching of another satellite in its "Kosmos" program. This was number one hundred and twelve in the series which began in 1962, and which by 1981 would reach serial number thirteen hundred.

The students suddenly realized that there was something odd about the schedule of this particular Kosmos payload, when they inspected their tapes and maps. When they traced its orbital path back to its first revolution around the earth, the "ground track" (of the sub-satellite point) carried it far to the west of either Baikonur, Tyuratam, or the Volga River site. This new satellite must have come from a point in northwestern Russia, but beyond drawing a line across the region, the schoolboys could not be more specific.

The Russians, of course, gave no indication that anything was unusual about the satellite. Today, while Plesetsk is the world's busiest space launch center, Moscow has still not even hinted at its existence.

Later in 1966, meanwhile, the Kettering schoolboys noticed new launchings from the mystery site, but on slightly different azimuths. This meant that the line of the original orbital revolution would intersect the lines plotted earlier. The lines were charted, and "X marked the spot:" the small town of PLESETSK.

Many kinds of satellites are launched from Plesetsk, more than one every week, week after week, year after year. But most go up in the daytime (photo spy satellites can't see in the dark), and the local inhabitants are accustomed to the noise and fire in the sky: no TASS reporter is going to make a sloppy mistake in this neck of the woods! Only rarely is a shot made at night into a high "lofted" trajectory—and when that happens, too many people see it. "Jellyfish UFO" sightings have occurred again in northwest Russia, on June 14, 1980 (Kosmos-1188) and May 16, 1981 (Meteor 2-7).

Some Plesetsk satellites are weather satellites, and others are communications satellites. Targets for satellite "hunter-killer" test are launched from here. Navigation satellites and other military support payloads also put into orbit from Plesetsk. Radar and microwave eavesdropping satellites are also seen (that was the mission of Cosmos-955).

But the most common is the "photo spy satellite," of which thirty to forty are shot into space every year. This is what happens on such a mission.

The twelve thousand pound satellites are constructed in three modules. The middle spherical module weighs about three tons, and used to be the 'command module' for cosmonauts. Behind it is a roughly tapered cylindrical "service module" which houses the satellite's retro-rocket and batteries. In front of the sphere is a disc-shaped 'hitch-hiker' satellite which can be an auxiliary payload such as a scientific probe or an additional maneuvering engine.

At blastoff, the giant booster rocket generates more than a million pounds of thrust from its five units of engines, each unit contained four main thrust chambers and a series of smaller control engines. After several minutes of flight, the four auxiliary rocket units exhaust their fuel and fall free while the center sustainer stage continues. It runs out of fuel on the edge of space, and an upper stage fires for several minutes to place the payload into a low orbit of the earth, between one hundred and two hundred miles high.

For up to thirteen days, this satellite circles the earth every eighty-nine minutes. Ground commands from a 'Mission Control Center' somewhere in Russia program the satellite's cameras to point and photograph specific locations on the ground. It could be an American air field, a British naval base, the Israeli border, a Chinese missile test range, a Japanese industrial area, or the Alaska pipeline. Frame by frame, the satellite collects its spy data.

Nobody really knows just HOW good the photos are, but experts speculate. Reportedly, American spy cameras in space can detect human figures on the ground. Aircraft tail numbers are, just possibly, readable. Russian cameras are not as good, nor is their film, but they can certainly keep track of deployment of ships, planes, and probably army divisions. They can certainly monitor activity and construction at supply and manufacturing facilities.

After two weeks, the satellite lines up backwards to its direction of motion and fires its rocket for the last time. Plummeting towards the atmosphere, the spherical section detaches and turns its heat shield forward, while the other modules are torn apart during the fiery re-entry.

The three-ton sphere falls through the air, releasing a series of larger and larger parachutes, and finally drifts to the ground in Soviet Central Asia, near the town of Karaganda. Helicopter crews rush up to the capsule, extract the precious film (each mission costs several tens of millions of dollars), and send it to a top secret photo-interpretation center for processing.

This basic spacecraft, which is manufactured at a secret location, has been used in over *five hundred* space missions over the past twenty years, a third from Tyuratam and two-thirds from Plesetsk. A few of the early shots carried cosmonauts, and were publicized under the Vostok and Voskhod programs. But the later shots were concealed under the label of the "peaceful, scientific, space exploratory" program called "Kosmos." A space secrecy curtain has been draped over this program for many years. Recently, a new-model space spy satellite based on the unmanned Soyuz vehicle has been introduced. It can spend up to six weeks in space, so fewer launches are going to be needed.

The notoriety of the Petrozavodsk UFO has attracted many tourists to the town, according to local newsmen. The Russian

UFO buffs arrive hoping to witness one of the many alleged "returns" of the alien jellyfish—but if they mount expeditions with cameras and other scientific gear, they must all return empty handed, since no new data has been reported about the local sensation.

Private travel to Petrozavodsk is yet another reason why Soviet officials seem to be every more nervous about their out-of-control UFO story. It seems that Petrozavodsk is a major staging area for the anti-Soviet "underground railway" which smuggles political refugees out of the country via the poorly guarded frontier with northern Finland. The latest resistence figure to take that route was Lithuanian dissident Vladas Sakalys, a thirty-eight-year-old optician from Vilnius who had spent fifteen years in Soviet labor camps for 'nationalist' sentiments. Again threatened with arrest in the spring of 1980, he took a train to Leningrad, then to Petrozavodsk and thence to the small town of Idel, where he walked and swam his way to safety in Sweden (if captured in Finland, the Finnish authorities would have turned him back over to the Soviet border guards.) Sakalys quite properly made no mention of the local help he must have received along this escape route—but his exploit and others like it are only one more headache for Soviet state security organs who must monitor the innocence of the many "UFO buffs" travelling to Petrozavodsk...to insure that they don't keep travelling!

Here is a UFO case witnessed by hundreds, if not thousands of people, who have been recounting and retelling their stories for more than three years without outside interference. Here is a UFO case for which we can be quite certain of the actual stimulus. So, if UFOlogists wish to tackle this opportunity, here is a chance to calibrate eyewitness testimony against a known baseline, in order to estimate how reliable similar testimony might be in other cases for which the original stimulus remains obscure. The situation as it stands now looks pretty hopeless, in that an honest appraisal of the eyewitness accounts as now being documented would probably be totally insufficient to reconstruct the actual original stimulus.

The moral, then, is that many of the "classic" UFOs that remain unexplained could well be based on prosaic stimuli for which the eyewitness perceptions (and embellishments) have become too garbled for an accurate reconstruction. The fact that they are unexplained proves nothing about the UFOs, but further underlines the problem of proving that "no earthly explanation" will serve for some UFO cases. So far that has yet to be proved.

AFTERWORD
UFO Research—Estimate
of the Situation
(1980 Smithsonian UFO Symposium Lecture)

As far as what we've learned in the past third of a century or so of research into UFO sightings: We've learned that people will see UFOs, whether or not extraordinary stimuli are there. For example, imagine a full one year's time in which the real UFOs (if they exist) stopped coming, went away and put up a reserved sign around the planet. Would we notice diminished reports and be able to detect their absence? Or wouldn't we still receive substantial numbers of reports, possibly almost as many sightings as before. Wouldn't we still have photographs? Wouldn't we still have numerous accounts of close encounters from people? Wouldn't we still have all the same types of evidence we do now? The nocturnal lights, the daylight discs, the mysterious power failures? We know what the ordinary richness of stimuli in our environment can cause. Such sightings will continue, and people will therefore keep seeing them. So I'd like to suggest that if removing this postulated, extraordinary cause (that is, "true UFOs") results in a situation which is indistinguishable from one in which it does not exist; then UFOlogists have to recover their whole case and try a different approach—since UFOs *need not* even exist.

We've learned that people will believe in UFOs. We already know that, for various reasons. For one, belief in UFOs is exciting, it's interesting. In many ways UFO research is the last resort of the citizen-scientist, who can go in the field. A hundred years ago there were many amateur scientists, people who dabbled in chemistry, geology, and the other sciences—each with their own experimental set-up. Nowadays science is almost a preserve of the big science businesses. And only in a few areas, some of the natural sciences, some areas of observational astronomy and UFO research can people really participate in a scientific process. And for the best of reasons, people enjoy that.

We've learned that statements such as "Either there's something up there or all these people are crazy" are illogical, the fallacy of the excluded middle. There are plenty of reasons why the majority of the percipients are honest, sober, clear-sighted people who are being genuinely puzzled, baffled, even frightened by phenomena that we find out are perfectly mundane.

We've learned, and it's been proven for us courtesy of the Center for UFO studies, that the much maligned Air Force project Blue Book provided very excellent statistics as far as solved and unsolved cases. The percentage of unknown cases in Blue Book was verified by Dr. Hynek's group several years ago. The Air Force was not explaining things away on a general basis. On a case by case basis we can find cases that do lend themselves to that interpretation, but in general the Air Force percentages stood the test of time. Twenty years later, now, we're a lot smarter in finding out what causes UFO reports and how people can sometimes be fooled into perceiving UFOs.

We've also learned that some witnesses can be identified as potentially unreliable, and I would quote, for example, from Dr. Hynek again: "The idea that one person, often with little understanding of statistics or probability, can have dozens of UFO sightings while a great many other people, indeed the majority, have never in their lives seen anything resembling a UFO, can instantly be shown to be utterly nonsensical." In other words, people who are repeatedly seeing UFOs are unreliable observers. Kenneth Arnold, for example, mentioned frequently as a very good UFO witness, has seen UFOs a dozen times, according to his own accounts. Betty Hill, who helped bring to prominence UFO close encounters and abductions, has seen UFOs dozens or is it hundreds of times? But, of course we are told to believe that her first sighting is reliable because it was confirmed under hypnosis as her later ones were not.

And we've learned more about hypnosis as well. People under hypnosis will tell UFO abduction stories that are undistinguishable from the stories of so-called "real abductees"— just like the ones Betty Hill and others have come up with. We didn't know this a few years ago; but we know it now. There have been suggestions that "false" abduction stories told under hypnosis are different from real ones; but I suggest there are only differences in the selection of witnesses.

We know as far as a person's criminal record or whatever is concerned—it's not relevant to his testimony; but in some famous cases the fact that people have lied about past criminal records and passed polygraph tests while doing so is highly relevant to the validity of their UFO testimony under the lie-detector.

We've learned, for example, that old cases are not particularly useful as sources of investigation: After twenty or thirty years people's memories are not what they were. Even a few days passing can hopelessly scramble crucial data in human memory banks. The things people remember are no longer accurate.

And the trails have long gone cold for any research. The kind of tools which today are used to solve modern UFO sightings cannot be applied to old cases. They are invulnerable to solution. One particular case I mentioned in *OMNI* in September 1980—I was called upon by a reader to research Gordon Cooper's sighting in Germany in 1951, involving flights of UFOs passing over his Air Force base. Now I have been researching that particular case for more than two years, checking the Air Force unit's historical files, (they're declassified), checking with other people in the unit, checking Blue Book files and other Air Force units, checking police records in Munich, even checking the UFO groups and newspaper files in Munich. And there is absolutely no record of anything of that sort ever happening that summer, except for Gordon Cooper's recollection—and *now* he doesn't want to talk about it with me.

. I submit that such research is never published because it's negative; and I think it likely either Cooper is remembering something else or misinterpreting what he remembered. And please, if you have anything on it, come to me; it's still an open case, still genuinely "unidentified." But useful? Not a chance.

We've learned more about hoaxes, too. You can't second-guess hoaxers. For we can't look at a person and say "He wouldn't lie to me because he's an honest person and has a good reputation. He has no motive for lying. And besides, he couldn't. The case could not be falsified." Well, that's really restricting our imagination. What we're saying is that no one else can do something that we can't quickly think of how to do ourselves. And also, people *will* commit UFO hoaxes. About 1% of sightings we've learned, not more, are hoaxes, although some of the most famous cases seem to be hoaxes. The problem is that you can not look at a case and say it couldn't be a hoax, because he had no rationale—he didn't behave the way a hoaxer would. The fact is, it's devilishly difficult to second-guess these people. I think we all know that by now; so we're a lot less confident, when it comes to smoking out hoaxes, than we used to be.

As far as the ETI hypotheses, extra-terrestrial spacecraft, I'm one of the people who think that interstellar travel is likely, feasible, something we're going to do. I wouldn't be surprised to see the first unmanned probes launched out of our solar system during my lifetime. I know my grandfather, who was my age when the first aircraft went up, said that he never expected to see people on the moon either—and they were. So we can play that game: Interstellar travel *is* possible; extraterrestrial civilizations *are* possible. Anyone who says he knows one way or the other is just blowing smoke because we don't know the factors involved. There could be alien civilizations visiting us in the solar system. I know of no *a priori* reasons against it, and I will not attempt to say that it cannot happen because of distances or technologies or whatever. And the number of visits involved? Some of the investigations of possible star travel of our descendents, grandchildren, say, suggest that robot probes can be sent and make a hundred year trip and, once they arrive, replicate themselves or build more scout ships. So, many arguments which people use as *a priori* against the extraterrestrial hypothesis, I don't think are valid. At the same time we seem to have our hands at the wrong end of the puzzle. The question is not *is it possible?* But whether the sightings we currently have prove that it is true. And the answer to this, I think, is 'no.' It has not yet proved that these reports are the result of such visitors. The fact is there could be undetectable visitors amongs us wondering if the UFO reports we are getting from each other represent a third party poaching— because they know it's not *them* that we're seeing.

So in conclusion, I will keep my eyes on the stars. If there are to be interstellar voyages, I think we are going to have to do it ourselves—but the UFO phenomenon has convinced people that it *might* be possible to do. So let's do it.

Appendix I

Supplementary UFO bibliography (supplemental, that is, to any printed in pro-UFO books, of which even the most rational (such as Hendry's) still impose a strict blackout on anti-UFO books they don't want their readers to see, while also containing pro-UFO books, even if they're garbage). Note: The authors are *not* necessarily all skeptics!

Cazeau, Charles, and Scott, Stuart, *Exploring the Unknown,* Plenum, New York, 1979 (not really a UFO book, but similar).

Cohen, Daniel, *The World of UFOs,* J. R. Lippincott, Philadelphia, 1979 (for younger readers, too).

Cohen, Daniel, *Creatures from UFOs,* Pocket Books, 1979.

Condon, Edward U., et al., *Final Report of the Scientific Study of Unidentified Flying Objects,* Dutton, New York, 1969, (reportedly out-of-print, but copies can always be obtained from the National Technical Information Service, Springfield, Virginia).

Frazier, Kendrick, *Paranormal Borderlands of Science,* Prometheus, Buffalo, New York, 1981.

Hendry, Allan, *The UFO Handbook,* Doubleday, New York, 1979.

Haines, Richard F., (ed.), *UFO Phenomena and the Behavioral Scientist,* Scarecrow Press, Metuchen, New Jersey, 1979.

Haines, Richard F., *Observing UFOs*, Nelson-Hall, Chicago, 1980.

Klass, Philip J., *UFOs Explained*, Random House, New York, 1974.

Kusche, Lawrence, *The Bermuda Triangle Mystery—Solved*, Harper & Row, New York, 1975 (not a UFO book, but related nonsense).

Menzel, Donald H., and Taves, Ernest H., *The UFO Enigma*, Doubleday, Garden City, NY, 1977.

Ridpath, Ian, *Messages from the Stars*, Harper and Row, New York, 1978.

Sagan, Carl, and Page, Thornton, *UFOs: A Scientific Debate*, WW Norton, New York, 1972 (also, Cornell University Press).

Sheaffer, Robert, *The UFO Verdict*, Prometheus, Buffalo, 1981.

Smith, Marcia S., *The UFO Enigma*, Congressional Research Service report 76-52 SP, Washington, D.C., 1976 (available from National Technical Information Service, Springfield, Va.)

Smith, Marcia S., *Extraterrestrial Intelligence and Unidentified Flying Objects: A Selected, Annotated Bibliography*, CRS Report 76-35 SP, Washington, D.C., 1976 (see above).

Appendix II

Where to write for periodic UFO news updates:

Skeptical Inquirer
Committee for the Scientific
Investigation of Claims of the
Paranormal (CSICP)
Box 229
Central Park Station
Buffalo, NY 14215

UFO Subcommittee, CSICP
1341 Poe Lane
San Jose, CA 95130

Mutual UFO Network
103 Old Towne Road
Seguin, TX 78155

Center for UFO Studies
Box 1402
Evanston, IL 60204

FATE Magazine
500 Hyacinth Place
Highland Park, IL 60035

Frontiers of Science
2201 St. Paul Street
Baltimore, MD 21218

UFO Review
(Timothy Green Beckley)
303 Fifth Ave., Suite 1306
New York, NY 10016

Flying Saucer Review
West Malling
Maidstone, Kent
Great Britain,

Dr. Bruce Maccabee
Fund for UFO Research
10706 Meadowhill Road
Silver Spring, MD 20901

Saucer News
James Moseley
Box 163
Fort Lee, NJ 07024

About the Author

James E. Oberg is a Phi Beta Kappa and graduated *summa cum laude* from Ohio Wesleyan University in 1966, with honors in mathematics and Russian. As a student he was a member of the five-time winning GE College Bowl team. He has worked as a computer analyst on laser weapons systems for the Air Force; as an instructor and curriculum developer at the Department of Defense Computer Institute in Washington, D.C., and at NASA's Lyndon B. Johnson Space Center, Houston; first in payload software development; then as Mission Control support for Approach and Landing test of the space shuttle "Enterprise." He works for McDonnell Douglas in NASA Mission Control, in 1981 as a member of the Ascent Team, specializing in computer control of orbital maneuvering system rockets and attitude control rockets on the shuttle "Columbia" and currently as a specialist in orbital rendezvous. He is a member of the American Institute of Aeronautics and Astronautics, the British Interplanetary Society, the Committee for the Scientific Investigation of Claims of the Paranormal (and is a co-founder of their UFO subcommittee), the National Space Institute, the L-5 Society (of which he is a former director), the National Association of Science Writers, and the Mutual UFO Network. He has received the AIAA Distinguished Lecturer Award, the National Space Club's Robert Goddard Space History Essay Award, and the Cutty Sark UFO Scientific Paper Award. His previous books include *Red Star in Orbit,* which *The New York Times Book Review* called "a stunning tour-de-force," and *New Earths,* a Book of the Month Club Science Alternate. His column, "UFO Update" appeared bi-monthly in *Omni* magazine, and he has written for *True, Star & Sky, The Los Angeles Times, Starlog, National Defense, Science & Mechanics, Technology Review, Analog, Destinies, New Scientist, Odyssey, Fate, Science Digest,* and *Space World.* Mr. Oberg lives with his wife and son on a twenty-two acre ranch in rural Galveston County, Texas, with a number of dogs, cats and half-Arabian horses. At six feet, eight inches tall it is no wonder his head is in the stars.

Acknowledgements

However unique and original the investigations in this book, it is still dependent on encouragement, aid, and critiques from colleagues-in-research. Foremost among them are fellow-skeptics Philip J. Klass and Robert Sheaffer, along with Elmer Kral, Thornton Page, David Schroth, Ian Ridpath, Allan Hendry, Jim Moseley, and George Earley. Guidance also came from my numerous editors, including J. Anderson Dorman, Jerome Clark, Kendrick Frazier, Ben Bova, Ray Palmer, Dennis Hauck, Herbert Furlow, Gene Wright, Harry Belil, Marty Singer, and Russ Rueger.

Special appreciation is expressed to Kathy Keeton for the 1979 OMNI UFO Summit, to Russ Taylor and Lindsay Ramsey for the Cutty Sark UFO Essay contest, and to Fred Durant for the 1980 Smithsonian UFO Symposium.

I received invaluable assistance from Richard Underwood (space photos), Terry White and Charles Redmond (NASA public affairs), Farouk El-Baz (National Air & Space Museum), Del Kindschi (North American Aerospace Defense Command), Ed Krupp, Ron Oriti, and Paul Rocques (Griffith Observatory, Los Angeles), Fran Waranius, Dan Kinsler and Stephen Tellier (Lunar and Planetary Institute, Houston).

My primary gratitude is to my wife Cooky, whose encouragement and constructive criticism has helped me focus my research activities on areas of greatest promise and benefit.